RED LIGHTNING BOOKS

BEER

Fest

USA

———— ✦ ∙∙∙∙ ✦ ————

CELEBRATING
AMERICAN CRAFT BREWS

M. B. Mooney

This book is a publication of

RED LIGHTNING BOOKS
1320 East 10th Street
Bloomington, Indiana 47405 USA

redlightningbooks.com

*Manufactured in the
United States of America*

Cataloging information is available
from the Library of Congress.

ISBN 978-1-68435-142-8 (hardback)
ISBN 978-1-68435-141-1 (paperback)
ISBN 978-1-68435-143-5 (ebook)

First printing 2021

CONTENTS

CRAFT BEERS

FOREWORD

BEER FESTIVALS ARE NOTHING NEW, AS EVIDENCED BY THE MUNICH Oktoberfest, which celebrated its 186th anniversary in 2019. But unlike the German tradition, beer festivals in the United States rarely commemorate a royal marriage. Instead, they celebrate the past thirty-five years of craft brewing in all parts of the world.

The emergence of local brewers has allowed for a wide variety of beer styles, which has helped educate the public to understand the difference between locally brewed ales and commercially produced traditional lagers. A beer festival is an excellent way for brewers to showcase these styles and gain valuable feedback from the folks who drink them. Perhaps most importantly, beer festivals promote friendship.

There seems to be a beer festival nearly every weekend, celebrating a season or a region or a style. Some beer festivals feature judging of beer styles, while others allow beer enthusiasts to personally rate beers by individual preference and share with their followers on social platforms.

My first experience with a beer festival in Oregon was the Mount Angel Oktoberfest, which started in 1966. The local German community is still producing this event with great success. Ten years later two friends and I attended the Munich Oktoberfest, where we joined Germans at their table and experienced the hospitality of perfect strangers with the common thread of beer and friendship.

The Oregon Brewers Festival began in 1988, when three local brewers obtained a permit from the City of Portland to use the waterfront park to showcase craft beers, along with nineteen other brewers from Alaska, California,

Montana, Oregon, Washington, and Wisconsin. According to the late beer writer Fred Eckhardt, "The Oregon Brewers Festival was to be a grand showing of America's finest new-wave 'micro-brewed' beers. This was to be an entirely new approach to beer festivals. These entrepreneurs had invited a whole range of America's smallest and most innovative brewers to bring their best to Portland's beautiful Waterfront Park on the banks of our Willamette River."

The first Oregon Brewers Festival far exceeded expectations with its success. This event spawned numerous other beer festivals to help promote craft brewing worldwide.

I hope you enjoy reading this book and appreciate the connection between beer festivals and friendship. The best beers are the ones we drink with friends.

Cheers!
Art Larrance

CRAFT BEERS

ACKNOWLEDGMENTS

FIRST, I NEED TO GIVE A HUGE AMOUNT OF GRATITUDE TO THE MEN and women who gave their time and effort for interviews. Each conversation was full of grace and generosity, and every single person taught me more about the industry and what it means to do something with passion and meaning. This book would not have happened without them.

My agent, Cyle Young, came to me with an idea, and that idea became two. I am thankful for his friendship and guidance on this journey.

The staff of editors at Indiana University Press has been amazing. I am thankful for their patience and professionalism during the whole process.

I'm grateful to my wife, Becca. Most people will see my name on the front of the book but not realize that her support, encouragement, and patience helped make it all possible. I'm the richest man I know.

Last but not least, I give thanks to God. Some people will find it strange to see God's name mentioned in a book about beer, but nothing good happens in my life without his blessing, and I am that—blessed.

CRAFT BEERS

Introduction

"O'Zapft is!"

In 1950, Munich mayor Thomas Wimmer grabbed a wooden hammer and opened the first barrel of beer at Oktoberfest that year. It took him seventeen blows with that hammer to get the barrel open, the longest in the modern Oktoberfest era. Once successful, he shouted, "O'Zapft is," which signaled the dancing and entertainment to begin. The technical translation is, "It's tapped!" In other words, "Let's party!"

It had been a rough couple decades. The Nazi flag had replaced the Bavarian one in 1933; by 1939, World War II had consumed Germany, putting festivals like Oktoberfest on hold. The war ended in 1945. The following year, Munich had an Autumn Festival instead of the traditional one celebrating Bavarian culture.

Although the horrors of war and national defeat were still fresh in everyone's mind, those in Munich recaptured their culture, celebrating a region and tradition that long predated world wars and the evil of Nazism. They reclaimed it through Oktoberfest, a celebration of culture, entertainment, and beer.

Oktoberfest began in 1810, when the whole city of Munich was invited to a royal wedding party in the fields outside the city gates. What started with horse races grew to include beer stands that developed into large beer tents by 1896. Enterprising landlords and local breweries set up beer halls to showcase one of Germany's favorite pastimes: drinking beer.

Since its beginning, it has grown into one of the biggest parties in the world. Oktoberfest is now more international than ever, with visitors of all ages; it boasts roller coasters and carousels, concerts and costume processions. People wear traditional Bavarian clothes—dirndls, lederhosen, and more—and now fourteen massive beer tents exist for people to explore, sitting at tables, eating German food, and drinking amazing beer.[1]

BEER IN AMERICA

When Germans began emigrating to the United States, America had a complicated relationship with beer. The only beer Americans knew was English ale, a dark and heavy brew that turned sour quickly; as a result, ale was a distant third to cider and spirits among the American drinkers. Since most drinking was with harder spirits and whiskey, alcohol developed a reputation as being for either the socially elite (brandy) or those wanting to simply get drunk at sketchy places, an idea supported by the rich and strict Christian religious heritage in the United States.

The German culture didn't make such associations. Beer was a necessity, an expression of their heritage; it was paired with food and social events in family-friendly affairs. When German immigrants arrived on American shores, the immigrants were hardworking, entrepreneurial people, taking the promise of opportunity seriously. And they loved their beer. These hardy folk moved into the Midwest, and when they didn't find the lagers they loved, they started brewing. And once they started brewing, they found other Americans (both of German descent and not) who wanted to buy their brews.

German immigrants brought more than just their recipes and business sense. For them, there was a whole culture around beer, including beer gardens, where a family could take the kids and the dog and have a beer and socialize. There, the beer was low in alcoholic content but full of flavor.[2]

Beer helped shape human history, serving as payment for the slaves building Egyptian pyramids, alleviating the worldwide problem of diseases in water by giving people something safe to drink, and helping Louis Pasteur discover the existence of bacteria.[3] In America, the booming beer industry was no different. Most brewers could only serve those a few miles away, but soon those small German American industrialists helped develop commercial refrigeration and bottling solutions. It was a perfect storm of opportunity and creativity during a period when inventions were changing lives. Great-tasting and safe beer spread all over the United States.

Some of these men became the biggest brewers in the country—Busch, Pabst, and Miller among them. As the passion for beer in America grew and the bigger companies became more competitive, the relationship between beer and Americans became more complicated. Anti-German sentiments of the early 1900s and the reform movement called Temperance combined in another perfect storm, and hundreds of breweries closed down. Even the big names like Busch and Miller stayed afloat only by investing in other enterprises, switching to sodas, or selling illegally through the 1920s.[4]

By the time the country had emerged from Prohibition and the Great Depression, only a handful of breweries remained. Those few embraced a dominating form of capitalism and became powerhouses of bottling and canning for the masses—cheaper beer for the bars and the home refrigerator.

THE CRAFT REVOLUTION

But some began to rediscover the old ways. Whether their interest arose from traveling to Germany and Europe or developing a new love of imported beer over the old, tasteless American stuff, people in the United States began to experiment with brewing beer and then opening local craft breweries in the 1970s and '80s. They discovered a passion for a great-tasting beer made from high-quality ingredients—quality over quantity.

The rediscovery of brewing great beer in homes and local breweries led to a new appreciation of that old culture of the beer garden and the taproom. What formed was a community of people out for an experience and connection not only with each other but also with the brewmasters. The natural next step was to celebrate great beer in a festival.

The brewing community is a unique set of people. While good business practices are important, equally vital, if not more so, are the passion for great beer and the skill to produce it. There is rivalry, but nowhere is there more collaboration between similar businesses than in the craft brewing industry. And the main point of competition is simple: Who can make the better beer?

So they celebrate their passion for great beer in a big festival.

This explosion of beer festivals didn't happen overnight. It began with a young homebrewer who wrote the bible on experimentation with brewing beer in garages and basements and kitchens and who had the initial idea for an American beer fest while visiting one in England. Then more places around the United States appeared to celebrate craft beer in big cities and small towns.

Every beer has a story. One of the attractions of a local craft brewery is the ability to ask the brewer how he or she developed the recipe. Enthusiasts seek out the story of the brewer as much as that of the brew.

Like the Oktoberfest of the German culture, beer fests are about more than beer. They are celebrations of local culture and styles of beer. They include music and friendly competitions. They have their own history and personalities. Most make very little money, but many have become launching points for breweries and other businesses to realize their dreams and passions. Core volunteers come back every year because of positive experiences and love of the event. Many of the festivals give back to the local community through charities or other means.

Like the craft beers at the festivals, these beer fests have their own stories, in states where politics, history, and the region exert influence. It is a story of immigration and anti-immigrant sentiments, of cultural clashes.

Prohibition tried to kill alcohol in 1919, and craft beer is the story of the resurrection of a whole culture, adapted and improved for the American consumer tired of the cheap, tasteless shrink-wrapped corporate brews and looking for a local experience that celebrates the old and new of great beer.

This book is about beer fests, but it is about more than that. It is a celebration of the importance of community and quality, each unique in expression but committed to gathering people in a safe environment where they can have the best day of the year. It is about people.

I've included the oldest and the biggest beer fests. There are also small and newer ones.

I hope you sit back and read this book with a mug of your favorite brew in your hand (and I hope it didn't take you seventeen hits with a hammer to get it). Raise it high and say, "O'Zapft is!"

Let's party.

Patrons ready for the Suwanee Beer Fest.
Courtesy of Veugler Design Group.

CHAPTER ONE

Suwanee Beer Fest

Suwanee, GA

BEER CITY, USA

Our story in Suwanee begins with another mayor, Mayor Williams.

Randall Veugeler owned a business in town with his wife, Angela. He loved beer—not just any beer but great, well-crafted beer—and he traveled with friends to all the local beer fests in Georgia. Angela drove him and picked him up so that he got home safe.

In their hometown, Randall passed the Suwanee Town Center, a park area with shops, condos, and residences around it that was the location of numerous community events. People hung out and gathered there just for fun. He thought the Suwanee Town Center Park would be a great place for a beer fest.

He brought the idea to Angela, who had one condition: if he started his own festival, he wouldn't go to any other beer fests. He agreed.

The first step was to talk to the city of Suwanee. They met with Mayor Dave Williams and pitched the idea of using the town center green to put on a great beer fest.

After the pitch, Williams responded by calling in one of the people on staff with the city, Denise, since she heard him often talk about his love for beer. He asked Denise, "What have I always wanted Suwanee to be?"

Her answer was immediate. "Beer City, USA."

Just as Mayor Wimmer did in Munich, Williams and the city staff opened the door to a community celebration of culture and beer. Randall and Angela, with their local company, the Veugeler Design Group, started building the Suwanee Beer Fest from the ground up.

In the original charter for the colony of Georgia in the 1700s, alcohol was illegal. James Oglethorpe was a prison reformer concerned with the over-crowding of England's debtors' prisons. This was a hopeless system where people went to prison if they couldn't pay off their debts, which resulted in the prisoners never being able to pay them off.

Oglethorpe got the charter for Georgia as a place for those people to pay off their debts as indentured servants, and many came there for that purpose. Oglethorpe didn't want more problems with these debtors, so he outlawed alcohol. Georgia was the only colony with that stipulation.

There was another problem, however: dysentery. People began getting sick and dying from drinking contaminated water. Major William Horton was Oglethorpe's second in command. While Oglethorpe was away back in England, Horton changed the law so that the people of Georgia could drink alcohol, especially beer, giving people something safe to drink. While upset with the change, Oglethorpe reluctantly agreed in order to save lives. Thus, beer actually saved the colony of Georgia.

The first brewery opened on Jekyll Island, initiated and built by Major Horton in 1738. Most cities soon had their own breweries because, in that time without refrigeration and modern transport, beer didn't make it far. Brewing became big business, and Atlanta and Savannah had several breweries.

Prohibition started earlier in Georgia and lasted even after the national event came and went. Georgia state laws kept alcohol illegal for years, and the Atlantic Brewery was the only one that survived.[1]

In 1978, President Jimmy Carter approved homebrewing, and soon local craft breweries began popping up, especially in the '90s. Places like Helenboch, Dogwood, Sweetwater, Red Brick, and more had times of success. However, a law in Georgia kept breweries from serving beer on-site, and this kept local craft breweries from growing in the state, unlike in Colorado and other places.[2]

KICKING IT OFF

When the Veugelers started the Suwanee Beer Fest in 2008, there were only thirteen craft breweries in Georgia. Randall called distributers and worked on getting breweries to the event. Suwanee Town Center was already a hub in the county, one of the first—and the most successful—town center areas

Bagpipes to open the festival. *Courtesy of Veugeler Design Group.*

in the Metro Atlanta suburbs. People came from all over the metro area for events and to eat and enjoy the great vibes.

Suwanee is a small local town, but it is known for its quality and atmosphere. Once the home of the Atlanta Falcons practice facility, it has been named one of the best places to live in the country (based on a metric including housing and schools) from sources such as *Money* and *Family Circle* magazines.

The Veugelers also owned the local *Suwanee Magazine*, so marketing the event to locals was a natural connection. They didn't think it would be that hard.

The first year was a disaster.

On July 30, 2011, twelve hundred people showed up for the first Suwanee Beer Fest. Tents and trailers full of beer populated the massive lawn area.

The crowd waiting to get into the festival. *Courtesy of Veugeler Design Group.*

Atlanta is known for its heat, and that day did not disappoint. The temperature climbed to 100 degrees that Saturday afternoon, and even the dedicated only made it through approximately half an hour before retreating. People left the town green and ducked into the air-conditioned restaurants near the park to get some relief.

The trailers damaged the grass. The beer fest ran out of cups. When they also ran out of water, people became dehydrated.

Yet visitors still had fun. Even though some called the event a disaster, most wanted to come back and do it again. They loved the celebration of Georgia breweries and craft brews from around the country.

MAY THE ROAD RISE TO MEET YOU

The Veugelers knew they had a lot of work to do to improve the event. Their first solution was to move it to March, coinciding with St. Patrick's Day. Their attempt to move the fest to a cooler time gave it more character. People arrived dressed in green and sporting other Irish-themed clothes. The Veugelers also got rid of the trailers that tore up the grass and switched to tent booths for the breweries and vendors.

Solving some problems brought up others. Now that the festival was in a cooler season and had more water, it ran out of bathrooms. The normal ratio for non–beer fest events was one portable bathroom for every 150 people. Suwanee Beer Fest doubled that, and it still wasn't enough. More people also showed up. The lines to get in were extremely long.

Despite the bathroom situation and the long lines, the local community loved the event. They were excited about the selection of beers.

The Veugelers found the secret to their success in a beer fest. They evaluated, adjusted, and made changes. Every year, the event improves and grows.

For example, in the third year, they added a corral—an area where people signed in, received their wristbands, and waited until the fest opened. This reduced the long lines for entering the festival but added another problem. A large group of people all came in at once, sampled the different kinds of beers, and then had to go to the bathroom all at once. Thousands of people acted as one—getting beer, going to the bathroom.

Another example is that they've mixed other vendors (such as a company that makes soap out of beer) in with the breweries, which improves the traffic flow.

SOMETHING FOR EVERYONE

Over the years, the event improved and grew to the point that they now have to cap the tickets at fifty-three hundred. Since there's nothing else on the calendar for St. Patrick's Day, it adds character to the event and makes branding easy. People show up with green shirts, suits, or hats. They might even dress like leprechauns.

The Suwanee Beer Fest is designed around the motto "something for everyone." Yes, it's about beer, but there is also food, entertainment, games, and more.

They brought in a few nonbrewery vendors and food options in the first year, but food trucks weren't as popular then as they are now. In 2019, the event had several food trucks offering a variety of choices.

A homebrew competition, in partnership with Brew Depot, began in the second year. Homebrewers from around the state enter the competition a week or two before the event. Judges are trained to rate beers strictly on the following criteria: mouth feel, aroma, appearance, flavor, and overall impression. Winners have gone on to be brewmasters at breweries in Georgia, notably Jekyll Brewery in nearby Alpharetta.

Costume competition. *Courtesy of Veugeler Design Group.*

There is a Georgia brew battle, where breweries in the state compete for the title of Georgia's best beer. When people register and get their wristbands, they also receive tokens. As people try the different brews, they can drop a token in a mug or receptacle to vote for their favorites. The Georgia brewery that gets the most tokens wins a big trophy and is celebrated. Past winners include Jekyll and Slow Pour in nearby Lawrenceville.

Because of the connection with St. Patrick's Day and the Irish and green themes, there is also a costume competition. Around the middle of the festival, those wanting to be in the competition sign up, and prizes are awarded in the categories of best beard, best costume (male and female), best kilt, and best-dressed couple. Winners get prizes from local shops and restaurants.

While there were only a handful of Georgia breweries in 2011, that number has grown. By 2013, there were thirty-three local breweries. Georgia changed the law in 2017, allowing breweries to serve the beer they produce on-site, and now there are more than eighty breweries in the state, a number that increases every week. In fact, Georgia only recently surpassed its pre-Prohibition number of breweries.

Due to the growth of craft brewing in the state, the Suwanee Beer Fest designated an area for those in Georgia, which turned into the Georgia Beer Garden in 2016.

GIGS AND JIGS

Live music has been a part of the festival from the beginning due to the convenient stage at the end of the town center green. Over the past few years, the event has featured local and regional bands such as the Rodeo Wins (rockabilly), Fulkinetic from Chicago, the Geeks Party Band, and the Pony League Band. Music goes on throughout the whole event, beginning with a bagpipe player who welcomes attendees every year when the event opens.

Slow Pour wins the Best Beer in Georgia.
Courtesy of Veugeler Design Group.

The Drake School, one of the most prestigious Irish dance schools in the United States, provides authentic Irish dancing. Their dancers have won awards at regional and national championships. Some are even world medal holders.

The Suwanee Beer Fest has a VIP tent for those who want a more exclusive experience. The VIPs get in the door an hour earlier than the general ticket holders and make their way to the designated area, where they enjoy a selection of thirty or more special brews and a catered meal. Of course, they can leave the VIP area and enjoy the other beers all around the lawn.

For more entertainment, attendees can play a giant Jenga or participate in cornhole. A local alehouse, Tannery Row in nearby Buford, sponsors the Tannery Top Dog, where participants ride a mechanical bulldog (in honor of the University of Georgia Bulldogs), and the winner is the one who lasts the longest. In 2018, the event added Xtreme AirBalls, a combination of a hamster wheel and a sumo suit in which people roll around the lawn, presumably after they've had a few samples of great beer for bravery.

AT THE END OF THE RAINBOW

Suwanee is a for-profit beer fest, but every year they give to local charities—over $100,000 dollars since 2011. They've given to the Wounded Warrior Project, a charity and veterans service organization dedicated to helping veterans wounded in military action since September 11, 2011 through programs and events.

For the last few years, the main supported charity has been Cooper's Crew Fund and the Cooper O'Brien Scholarship. Cooper O'Brien was a local student at North Gwinnett High School who developed a rare form of cancer, clear cell sarcoma. Tragically, he died from the disease, but his parents have kept his memory alive through generous giving. Cooper's Crew Fund raises money for research to cure childhood cancer, and the scholarship is given to North Gwinnett High School seniors who have overcome hardships and need help with college tuition.

TWO PEOPLE SHORTEN THE ROAD

The Suwanee Beer Fest has food, entertainment, games, breweries, and more, but none of it would happen without the volunteers. The volunteers have been the backbone of the event since its inception. April Miller, who helps administrate the festival, organizes more than 350 volunteers each year. She has developed a core group of one hundred who work like a family and come back every year. They recruit other volunteers for April because she makes it personal, knows people by name, and takes care of them.

The Veugelers try to add something every year to give the volunteers a great day, from a snack and pizza tent to shifts so that they can take breaks to a catered party in the office, sometimes with leftover beer. Randall had a garage full of leftover beer the first year, and what better way to get rid of it than by throwing a huge party for the volunteers?

The Suwanee Beer Fest is organized so that every tent has a selection of different brews. They even include other kinds of drinks for those who don't like beer; recently there was an alcoholic Mountain Dew that was particularly popular. It's part of their "something for everyone" motto.

The brewers give away stickers and other little items at their tables, all of it contributing to the vibe and the community.

Security for the event is a combined effort by the Suwanee Police and a private security company. Volunteers or security call if there's an issue, but it is such a family friendly event that there are rarely problems. People come with families and friends for a great day at the park. To encourage safety, Uber and Lyft offer discounts, and the beer fest provides shuttles to some local restaurants and accommodations to improve traffic and cut down on drinking and driving.

The festival is increasingly popular. Attendance has increased from twelve hundred in the first year to a current cap of fifty-three hundred. In one year, the VIP tickets sold out in three days. People come from all over Georgia and even all over the country to this little town. One man comes from California for the weekend to attend with family and friends. Another flies in from Seattle to meet up with his buddies. Big groups come together.

Irish dancers.
Courtesy of Veugeler Design Group.

THE LUCK OF THE IRISH

People can get good beer at any grocery store. Why do people spend fifty dollars or more for a few hours in the afternoon on a Saturday—and why do they come back every year?

People love the beer selection, all in one place. They get to try new beers, ones they would never encounter otherwise. In 2019, Suwanee had 101 breweries with 356 beers, and reps from the brewers come as well. Those who appreciate craft beer love to talk to the brewers or the reps about recipes and styles rather than to a volunteer who just pours the drinks. While a couple of international breweries have participated in the past, it is now an all-American beer fest.

People also love the venue. Suwanee Town Center has been successful and is constantly busy with events because it is a great, central spot that is easy to get to and that is structured for all kinds of activities, from concerts to 5K

Attendees sporting the St. Patrick's Day theme. *Courtesy of Veugeler Design Group.*

races and more. For the businesses around the town center, the Suwanee Beer Fest is the best business day of the year, as thousands of people descend on shops and restaurants before and after the festival.

The event is like being at a party with a group of close friends. There have never been any conflicts or fights.

One couple got engaged at the Suwanee Beer Fest. Businesses use it as a networking opportunity, bringing clients or staff to simply have fun together.

Randall and Angela strive to make it better every year and to bring value to the local community. Their pursuit of excellence in every area makes the difference, and the Suwanee Beer Fest has become one of the biggest and best in the state of Georgia and in the Southeast, continuing to grow and improve while others come and go.

With a passion for one of the greatest small towns in the United States, a love for great craft beer, and the support of the local community, the Suwanee Beer Fest is a safe and fun party where everyone is welcome, and people leave ready to come back every year.

Just remember to wear green.

What You Need to Know

EVENT Suwanee Beer Fest

WEBSITE https://suwaneebeerfest.com/

LOCATION Town Center Park, Suwanee, Georgia,
about thirty-five minutes northeast of Atlanta via I-85

FOUNDED 2011

DATES Mid-March

DESIGNATED DRIVER TICKETS AVAILABLE Yes

ADMISSION FOR THOSE UNDER TWENTY-ONE No

CHAPTER TWO

Great American Beer Fest

Denver, CO

THE PIONEER

There are pioneers, legends who have changed the face of the world, though we may not have heard of them. A young couple enjoying a local brew at their favorite new pub may not know the name of Charlie Papazian, but they are living in a community he helped create.

Papazian is from New Jersey. Young Charlie didn't drink beer because it didn't taste very good, but a neighbor introduced him to brewing his own beer. He and some friends concocted their first brews in the basement of a day care center, after hours. At the time, homebrewing was illegal, of course.

After he graduated from the University of Virginia with a degree in nuclear engineering in 1972, he and a friend drove to Colorado. He got a teaching degree at a local school in Boulder and worked on homebrewing in the evenings. Once friends caught word of his hobby, he began teaching others how to homebrew, and the book he later wrote, *The Complete Joy of Homebrewing*, became the brewing bible.

It was outlaw brewing. All homebrewers had were limited malts and simple methods, but compared to the cheap, mass-produced beer of the time, it tasted great. He started the Association of Brewers, which later merged with another organization to become the American Brewers Association.

Colorado was an outlaw state. Even though breweries were diminishing in Colorado, Boulder was ripe for craft brews. The country was ripe for them.

Ready to pour for the festival.
Courtesy of Brewers Association.

THE PIONEER STATE OF BEER

Colorado has a long history of brewing beer. During the Gold Rush of the mid-1800s, saloons weren't just places to drink. They were restaurants, hotels, social clubs, and even post offices. People came to the West to find wealth, land, and opportunity, and they were thirsty.

The first local barrel of beer was tapped in 1859 in Denver, and in 1873, Adolph Coors founded his brewery, nestled in the town of Golden, Colorado. He used fresh water from local mountain springs, and the locals called it "miner's bouquet." While Coors is the most popular brand, others, such as Zang and Tivoli, rose during the same time.[1]

Prohibition became state law in Colorado four years earlier than in the rest of the country and remained for more than a decade. But Prohibition couldn't kill the saloon culture. For example, Grahan's Saloon, a popular Denver drinking spot and poker hall, became Grahan's Soft Drink Parlor. People made their way to the basement, where the city's hottest speakeasy waited for them.

Most breweries didn't survive, though. Under the influence of men such as Papazian, homebrewing spread like wildflowers through word of mouth and clandestine meetings. After Prohibition, many of those homebrewers went pro, and now there's a local brewpub on every corner in the state.

From Prohibition to the present day, Colorado produced 1.9 million barrels of craft beer, making it third in the United States for sales and production of local brews. The state boasts over 280 breweries.[2]

Denver is known as the Napa Valley of Beer. It's a city filled with beer lovers, and more beer is brewed there every day than in any other US city. Fifteen brewpubs are housed downtown, including two of the nation's largest—Wynkoop and Rock Bottom. Beer is such a part of Colorado culture that one of Wynkoop's founders, John Hickenlooper, was elected governor of the state.

BIRTH OF A BEER FEST IN BOULDER

The city of Boulder, specifically, was already a cool spot in the 1970s and 1980s, home to great Olympic athletes and successful businesspeople. It was a community with a conscience, and talk of how to save the world was constant.

Papazian defined the craft brewing community, infusing it with his personality. He was a scientist and an artist, an educator and a collaborator. He

New Belgium Brewery booth. *Courtesy of Brewers Association.*

wanted to gather people to share his passion for great beer—not for guzzling but for responsibly enjoying the experience, taste, and quality of the craft. He wasn't focused on profit but believed that the community could grow beyond what others thought possible.

We see all these elements in the craft brewing community today. He created a culture with his personality and his love for craft brewing at its core.

Papazian's passion for beer didn't end in Boulder, thankfully. On a trip to England in 1982, he attended the Great British Beer Festival. In awe of the diversity and quality of beers, he turned to his friend and said, "Do you think you could ever have an event like this in the United States?"

His friend, popular British "Beer Hunter" Michael Jackson answered, "Yes, but where would you get the beer?" America wasn't known for making great beer, and the craft industry languished in its infancy, with only about forty breweries. But Papazian believed and put together the first Great American Beer Fest in 1982.

In the tradition of the Oktoberfest before it, the GABF is now one of the biggest parties in the world, holding the Guinness World Record for most beers on tap in one place.

Sample glass for the Great American. *Courtesy of Brewers Association.*

At the first GABF in 1982, however, only eight hundred attendees entered a Boulder hotel banquet room, which was set up with tables of six-ounce glasses for the two-ounce samples. There were twenty-four breweries and forty-seven beers.

Attendees learned about different kinds and styles of beers, compared porters with stouts and ales, and developed a new love affair with hops. The beers dazzled with their tastes and aromas. The crowd spoke with experienced homebrewers, who inspired several to return to their neighborhoods and start experimenting. There was a camaraderie between homebrewers and craft brewers, since they all retrofitted other equipment to use for brewing, such as using dairy tanks or other ingenious solutions.

Legendary early craft brewers attended, such as Ken Grossman from Sierra Nevada Brewing Co., Jim Schlueter from River City, Tom Burns and Al Nelson from Boulder Brewing, and others.[3]

In other words, they found the beer.

Bagpipes open the festival. *Courtesy of Brewers Association.*

THE MECCA OF BEER

It took more than passion to make the Great American what it became. Papazian and the craft industry were persistent and resilient, encouraging each other to do it even when no one was paying attention. They had to introduce people to great beer one beer at a time.

Two years passed, and the GABF needed more space. It moved from Boulder to the Merchandise Mart in Denver. It grew to seven thousand attendees in 1992 and kept growing. The event moved to the Denver Convention Center in 2000.

The GABF has become the mecca of beer in America.

In 2019, the thirty-eighth annual event, there were sixty-two thousand attendees, eight hundred breweries, and four thousand beers. While the organization of the breweries has changed and improved over time, they are now organized by nine regions: Great Lakes, Mid-Atlantic, Midwest, Mountain West, New England, Pacific, Pacific Northwest, Southwest, and Southeast.

Food trucks feed the population. *Courtesy of Brewers Association.*

The GABF has also grown to four different sessions—evening sessions on Thursday, Friday, and Saturday and an afternoon session on Saturday. It is the stage to highlight all that is great about beer and the craft community.

BREWERS AND VOLUNTEERS

Many reps and brewmasters come to the festival themselves. "Meet the Brewer" is a place where brewery founders gather and speak about the art of brewing. There are presentations from brewers such as Garrett Oliver and Ken Grossman. Even first-time brewers talk about their inspiration and styles. "Meet the Brewer" is part of the general ticket and always a favorite among attendees.

Four thousand volunteers help power and run the fest, including the Brew Crew, trained volunteers who pour drafts. There are many long-standing volunteers, and it is such a popular event that people can't simply sign up to volunteer. They must be recommended and invited. Such a high degree of interest ensures the quality of the volunteers and the event.

The volunteers are spread out among the different shifts and roles. They receive free tickets to the festival, and the volunteer coordinator works with them throughout the year and through other programs to train them and get them ready for the beer fest.

PAIRED WITH FOOD

Food trucks must be approved by the convention center. Their fare is for general consumption.

For something special, there is Paired, a side event and separate ticket with food and beer pairings to educate people in how meals and styles go together.

In Paired, an executive chef is on staff with the craft beer program. Breweries enter a lottery system to determine which beers will be served at Paired. These beers are not available anywhere else at the festival. The lead chef works with twenty-four award-winning chefs, mostly American, for this side event; they collaborate to create a menu. Each chef is assigned a beer and creates a dish for that beer. It's an amazing experience.

Paired is a special food and beer experience.
Courtesy of Brewers Association.

SECURITY AND SAFETY

As the event grew to tens of thousands of people, security became increasingly important. The GABF works closely with the City of Denver's public safety, police, and fire departments, and they hire a separate security contractor. The contractor works with other high-level events, such as the Olympics and the Super Bowl. It is familiar with large crowds and events with high-risk potential.

There have been no incidents in the history of the GABF.

Related to safety, the festival makes sure that everyone drinks responsibly and gets home safely. The GABF works with and promotes rideshare partners. Denver also has an amazing public transportation system, both light rail and bus. The festival sells designated driver tickets for the event and provides a Designated Driver Lounge, where the drivers can hang out, get free massages, make pottery, and more.

How do you provide bathrooms for sixty-two thousand people? The convention center has its own facilities, but the GABF rents many portable toilets and spaces them around the center. At this point, the events team has the bathroom management down to a science.

THERE'S GOLD IN THOSE HILLS

The celebration of beer includes some major competitions. The Great American has the largest commercial beer competition in the world, organized by styles. Getting a medal can be life changing for a small brewery.

In the Pro-Am competition, homebrewers work with professional brewers to scale up a recipe. This is judged as well, and there is a Best in Show award.

The American Homebrewers Association puts on the Great American. In a separate event in the spring, they host the National Homebrew Competition, which is also one of the largest beer competitions in the world.

Just like at any huge party, there's plenty of entertainment. Every session begins with a parade of bagpipers through the festival hall, bringing everyone in. On Friday, there is a Festival Flair Contest, where people dress up in costumes for prizes. There are karaoke events and music acts. The 2019 fest included Winter Wondergrass, a professional touring bluegrass act, on the stage.

Papazian has had fun with grand, flamboyant entrances to the Beer Fest. People look forward to giving him a fist bump. Bill Coors came to the fest in one of the early years and said it would change the face of the beer industry.

In 1985, at the American Homebrew Association conference, Papazian rode into the hotel ballroom on a circus elephant. He always innovates and has fun.

THE HEART OF A FESTIVAL

Papazian is proud of the positive and inclusive nature of the craft beer community and the GABF. People have a "we can do it too" experience because he believes anyone can brew his or her own beer. Drinkers and brewers are encouraged and inspired; they get support to continue their passion for great beer.

The GABF is always evolving, trying to be better every year. There is an attendee survey, and the organization takes that feedback seriously and changes operational details as needed, trying to keep the festival relevant.

The vision of the Great American is to be the premier beer fest in the world, the place to share and display all that is great about American beer.

The fledgling craft brew culture from the 1970s, mostly homebrewers, has come a long way in the past forty years. Charlie Papazian retired from the Brewers Association in 2018, but he still visits local breweries and is especially interested in ones off the beaten path. He is always in awe of the unique architecture and new brews that brewmasters create.

INNOVATION AND THE THOUGHTS OF A PIONEER

Innovation is a huge part of the craft beer community, which makes it interesting and unpredictable. At one time, fruit and honey beers were revolutionary. Now they are everywhere. In the early days, people were so starved for good beers that they loved them all. After forty years of massive growth, there are so many styles that there may be some you don't like!

Papazian is a national treasure. You can't often say that an individual has birthed and fostered a revolution. He did it quietly and calmly, a revolution without guns. As proof of his singular influence, the Smithsonian asked him for anything for their museum, and he gave them an old wooden spoon and trash can he used for brewing in the beginning of his homebrewing career.

Papazian told me via email that he estimates the rise of craft brewing has created more than one hundred thousand jobs. What about jobs related to the field? The industry needs grains, hops, and brewing equipment, not to mention barstools.

Music entertains the crowd. *Courtesy of Brewers Association.*

He scoffs at the notion that craft brews have saturated the market. They are currently at 12 percent of the beer industry. People have been saying the market is saturated for twenty years, and it still grows. Ever the optimist and dreamer, Papazian believes that there's potential for the craft market to double in the next few years.

For Papazian, it's about passion and dreaming, collaboration and innovation. It's about loving great beer. People entering the industry for selfish reasons won't last long. He should know. The community is his baby. It's not dedicated to getting drunk or wasted, drinking until the taste doesn't matter. It's a community where people drink responsibly, feel connected to their neighbors and local businesses, and welcome everyone around a shared experience.

Other countries model their festivals after the GABF, especially the Expo Cerveza Mexico. Fifteen years ago, Europeans thought the craft brew industry in America was laughable. Now even our friends in Europe recognize that America is leading the way in making great beer.

Since Papazian's retirement, others have taken on the mantle to make the Great American Beer Fest better every year. Records are broken, and more craft breweries appear every year. But even though the Great American gets bigger, at the core is a simple passion that always has room for one more beer lover. All you need to join is a friend and a great brew in your hand. Take your time. Slow down. Enjoy the quality and the flavors.

It's that simple. Changing the world, one brew at a time. What a revolution.

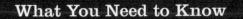

What You Need to Know

EVENT   Great American Beer Fest

WEBSITE   https://www.greatamericanbeerfestival.com/

LOCATION   Colorado Convention Center,
  700 Fourteenth St., Denver, CO

FOUNDED   1982

DATES   Usually late September or early October

DESIGNATED DRIVER TICKETS AVAILABLE   Yes

ADMISSION FOR THOSE UNDER TWENTY-ONE   Children under two,
  if carried by a parent at all times

The parade opens the festival. *Photo by Timothy Horn. Courtesy Oregon Brewers Festival.*

CHAPTER THREE

Oregon Brewers Festival
Portland, OR

THE PARADE

The Oregon Brewers festival starts on a Wednesday in July with a brunch hosted by one of the Oregon breweries, catering breakfast food for the five hundred people who attend. It is a separate ticket from the main event, and it sells out quickly. It starts at 9:00 a.m., and when it ends at 11:30 a.m., everyone goes out to the street and participates in a parade. The police escort the parade, which includes a band and a grand marshal. It takes about a half hour for the parade to make it to the Tom McCall Waterfront Park in downtown Portland, and others jump in along the way.

Once they arrive at the park, Art Larrance, one of the founders and head of the Oregon Brewers festival, introduces the charity of the year. He welcomes guest brewers, and then a representative from the brewery that hosted the brunch says a few words and chooses the one for the following year. Even though he isn't the mayor of Portland, in the tradition of the mayors of Munich at the Oktoberfest, Art Larrance taps a large barrel of beer made by the brunch host. Everyone who attends gets a glass from that first keg.

With that, the Oregon Brewers Festival, one of the oldest and largest in the United States, is open for four days.

FROM HOMEBREWER TO PROFESSIONAL

It all began thirty-three years ago with Art Larrance and other Portland brewers.

Larrance started as a homebrewer, brewing with friends in the later 1970s and early 1980s. The good beer they found in their city of Portland came from elsewhere, such as Washington and Vancouver. Why couldn't they start their own brewery?

Portland didn't have a bustling brew culture at the time. Charles and Shirley Coury worked in wine for years before opening the Cartwright Brewing Company in 1980 and producing a light ale. They closed in 1981 because the beer wasn't great, and the bottling was poor.

Along with a couple of friends interested in making great beer together, the Courys went to Yakima, Washington, to visit microbrewer Bert Grant. They asked him questions and worked out a consulting agreement for him to help build a small commercial brewery in Portland. Larrance and the others also licensed a few of Grant's recipes for brews. Portland Brewing began in 1984.

The problem was, however, that it was illegal to brew and sell on the same premises, a law that had been on the books since Prohibition. This kept breweries from starting brewpubs, which was the purpose of the law.

Wanting to see the craft brew culture grow in Oregon, three Portland breweries joined forces to change the law. Larrance and his partner, Fred Bowman of Portland Brewing; Richard and Nancy Ponzi of Columbia River; and Kurt and Rob Widmer of Widmer Brothers Brewing wrote the bill together.

Dick and Nancy Ponzi were part of a local wine family who teamed up with brewer Karl Ockert to establish Columbia River Brewery. Ockert was a graduate of the University of California's legendary Davis Malt and Brewing Sciences program. Columbia River set up shop in a three-story one-hundred-year-old former rope factory. Today it is known as Bridgeport Brewing.

Kurt and Rob Widmer also brewed at home so they'd have beer they wanted to drink. Homebrewing for themselves and their friends became a bigger and bigger hobby. Once they grew tired of the corporate gig, the brothers turned the hobby into a business. Like many of the early breweries, they used makeshift parts to pull together Widmer Brothers Brewing, with Kurt as the brewmaster.

Art Larrance and Fred Bowman opened Portland Brewing soon after. All three of these breweries were opened in 1984.

As the number of breweries grew, so did the cooperative spirit. Beer lovers naturally worked together to get the law changed for their industry, but it kept failing to pass state legislature. When they revised the legislation to also allow Coors beer to be sold in the state, their bill was finally successful in 1985.

Breweries began opening all over Oregon.

Like the experimental and innovative brews that soon dominated the numerous pubs, Oregon had the perfect mix for brewing—a pioneer spirit, a do-it-yourself mentality, a pervasive pub culture, and extensive fields for farming.

With more than one hundred breweries, Oregon is at the forefront of craft brewing and boasts one of the first two colleges in the country offering brewing as a major. Breweries in Oregon have won medals—too many to mention—at the Great American Beer Fest. Oregon is the second-leading producer of hops in America.

Flaming bagpipes! *Photo by Timothy Horn. Courtesy Oregon Brewers Festival.*

Beer brewing began in the early days of Oregon. Henry Saxter, a German immigrant, established the Liberty Brewery in 1852, but it was his successor who grew Liberty into a brewing powerhouse.

Henry Weinhard apprenticed as a brewer in Stuttgart, Germany. He left for America at the age of twenty-two in 1852. He arrived in New York in the pre–Civil War political conflict and knew that wasn't the place for him to start brewing beer. He made his way west, quenching people's thirst for great beer—first in Philadelphia, then in Cleveland and the state of Washington before finally settling in Portland, Oregon.

Weinhard and a partner, George Bottler, came to Portland in 1855 to compete with Saxter and Liberty Brewing. Portland proved to be an interesting opportunity. Farmers grew hops in the vicinity, and the city had thirsty loggers, dockworkers, and other laborers galore. After the company struggled, Weinhard bought out Bottler and Saxter to own Liberty Brewing outright.

He now owned the entire Portland brew trade. Liberty Brewing expanded and distributed across the United States and even to Asia.

Weinhard's success was interrupted—not by corruption, greed, or other common business mistakes but by progressive women, men, and politicians who were trying to make the world a better place by getting rid of alcohol.[1]

The Oregon Woman's Christian Temperance Union organized in 1883 at the First African Methodist Episcopal Church, just blocks away from Weinhard's brewery. From there, the Temperance movement spread across the state, often replacing brew taps with water fountains.

To mock the threat of Prohibition and the change to water fountains, Weinhard offered to pump beer through the new Skidmore Fountain at the center of Portland on its opening day. City officials politely declined.

Oregon has been—and still is—a progressive state of forward-thinking reformers. In the early 1900s, Prohibition was seen as needed progress. Temperance members were the reformers of the day, and alcohol became illegal in Oregon four years before it did nationally in 1919.

To survive those times, like others around the country, Weinhard merged with another brewer, Arnold Blitz's Portland Brewing Company, in 1928 and invested in other ventures. They eventually became the Blitz-Weinhard Brewing Company.

Fortunately, the days of Prohibition were soon over, but the Great Depression was in full swing, with a crashing stock market and high unemployment. "I think this would be a good time for a beer," Franklin D. Roosevelt said in 1932 when Prohibition was repealed.

For the next fifty years, only five breweries operated in Oregon—Blitz-Weinhard, Olympia, Rainier, Lucky Beer, and Heidelberg. Although all the beers tasted the same—and reportedly not that good—drinkers in Oregon stuck to their favorites with fierce loyalty.

It all started to change in the 1970s with homebrewing and craft beer. Unlike the microbrewing cultures in California and Washington, however, Portland's centered around the culture of brewpubs.[2]

THE FIRST YEAR OF THE OREGON BREWERS FESTIVAL

Art Larrance and his contemporaries entered the scene in the early 1980s. They were a cooperative and friendly group, and interest in craft beer increased in the state along with the number of breweries. As an indication of the popularity, the Papa Aldo's Blues Festival asked Larrance and Fred Bowman of the new Portland Brewing Company to sell beer at a festival at the waterfront park in July. They agreed, thinking they would sell sixteen or twenty kegs on the day.

The festival ran out of beer early. Larrance loaded ten empty kegs in his truck, raced to Portland Brewing, filled them up, and transported them back. By the time he returned from the brewery, the previous ten kegs were gone.

In the end, they sold seventy-six kegs, at three dollars for a twelve-ounce glass, and depleted the brewery's supply.

Papa Aldo's didn't want to repeat the festival and turned it over to the Blues Festival Association, but the permit was good for two years. The Blues Association didn't want that date, leaving it open for someone else.

Larrance had been to Oktoberfest in Munich. He saw what a huge party it was and wanted to re-create a similar atmosphere, exposing the public to great microbrews. He didn't want to make it a carnival like Munich was but wanted it to be similar in the exploration of new and unique beers people hadn't tried before.

The Great American had been the first US beer festival, and Larrance also didn't want to copy it. Whatever Great American Beer Fest did, he wanted to do the opposite—hosting it outside instead of inside, with no competitions, and limiting the number of beers.

Cheers to a great event.
Photo by Timothy Horn. Courtesy Oregon Brewers Festival.

Portland Brewing bought Papa Aldo's Blues Festival's permit, and Larrance approached his brewer friends in Portland for assistance. Kurt Widmer and Nancy Ponzi came to help. They set up the Oregon Brewers Association and started planning the first Oregon Brewers Festival.

Inexperienced with large events, they were "flying by the seat of their pants," Larrance said. They wanted to bring in beers from outside of Portland for local drinkers to compare and share what other brewers were doing in other parts of the country. The small team invited small and innovative brewers and not just the big names.

The festival was free for everyone to attend, including kids, but attendees bought plastic mugs. They were plastic rather than glass because the park bureau didn't want broken glass at the park. People got the mug for one dollar

Raise a glass to great beer.
Photo by Timothy Horn. Courtesy Oregon Brewers Festival.

and then paid another dollar for a half-pint serving or two dollars for a full. The Oregon Department of Agriculture sponsored the festival as an educational event, since so many were ignorant of the new industry, and they advised the Brewers Fest staff about signage and displays.

Larrance and the team got their friends and family to pitch in wherever possible. The Brew Crew, local homebrewers, organized and took over the volunteers.

The first Oregon Brewers Festival was held in 1988. Twenty-two breweries from six states came that first year, from Sierra Nevada to Triple Rock and others.

Larrance and the others estimated that five thousand people would attend on that first day.

More than fifteen thousand arrived, overwhelming the festival with the number of people. Problems arose. The limited coolers kept breaking down in the ninety-five-degree heat. Because of the cooler situation and the heat, the beer was foamy, and there wasn't enough. Local breweries had to make emergency runs for more beer to keep people drinking throughout the two days. The portable toilets ran over.

While it was a disaster in some ways, the attendees were well behaved and understanding, declaring that they enjoyed the event despite the glitches. Everyone was ready to do it again.

A SUCCESSFUL DISASTER

The festival added a third day in 1990. In 1993, the city asked the Brew Fest to move to the third weekend in the month. They added a second big tent in 1994 to make it more comfortable. Additional beer trailers were added to improve the wait times. The festival went to four days in 2005, and then five days in 2013, running from Wednesday to Sunday.

Larrance left Portland Brewing in 1994 and started another brewery, Cascade. He bought out Bridgeport and Widmer Brothers to manage the festival on his own.

To improve the taste experience and to be kinder to the environment, the Brewers Fest went to glass mugs in 2013, but the police department asked for a return to plastic for safety reasons. After changing from Thursday to Sunday for a few years, the festival returned once again a four-day festival, running from Wednesday through Saturday.

More than sixty thousand people attend the event, approximately eight thousand people at one time over the four days. In 2019 the fest featured ninety-two breweries, all from Oregon for the first time. This was a far cry from the struggles during Prohibition a century before.

INTERNATIONAL COMMUNITY

The intent and mission of the Oregon Brew Fest is to celebrate the open-handed brew culture that exists in countries around the world, not just in the United States.

Some patrons dress up in homage to Oktoberfest.
Photo by Timothy Horn. Courtesy Oregon Brewers Festival.

Eight years ago, Larrance received a call from Travel Portland, an organization that promotes tourism in the city. They explained that a sister city in the Netherlands had heard of the Oregon Brewers Fest and wondered whether a similar beer festival could work somewhere in Europe. Intrigued, Larrance went to the Netherlands and met the people at Moreland Brewery.

Instead of bringing the Brewers Fest to Europe, he invited ten Dutch breweries to come to the Oregon Brew Fest. He bought their beer and flew them over. Each of the ten was adopted by a Portland brewery, and these friendships continue today.

Larrance has also brought in breweries from Germany, New Zealand, Japan, China, Mexico, and other countries. He gathers those who are passionate about beer and encourages relationships with brewers, wherever they come from.

Tourists fly in from all over the world. The festival has a large map where people put pins in the cities they're from. It even has a pin in Antarctica!

SAFETY AND THE CITY

With any large event, volunteers are important, and the Oregon Brew Fest uses two thousand of them during the four days. Larrance keeps a list of former servers. They sign up online and choose shifts. People fly in to participate. Some come from Europe, especially from the Netherlands, and they get mugs and special T-shirts. Some volunteers have been involved for twenty-five years and are now old friends. Those who volunteer are appreciative of the event. Larrance recognizes them and heaps praise on them, hoping they'll come back next year to serve again.

Large events also require top security, and the Brew Fest is very conscious of keeping everyone safe. At peak periods, there are forty-four hired security personnel, along with six Portland police officers. Other supervisors and servers, each with a walkie-talkie on a communication system, are trained to keep an eye on the crowd and to help keep lines from getting too long. Since 9/11, the city instructed the event to increase security and detailed what should be built into the security, event management, and emergency management plans. For example, there are six emergency medical technicians (EMTs) now instead of the former two.

The Brewers Fest gives free taxi rides home for those who need them, and the waterfront park is along the river in the heart of Portland, with mass transit close by.

Friends enjoying a beer together. *Photo by Timothy Horn. Courtesy Oregon Brewers Festival.*

The focus of the festival is on the beer, so there isn't much entertainment. Bands are low-key, and kids can get their faces painted. Nondrinkers can hang out in the Root Beer Garden.

GENEROSITY AND FAMILIES

The event focuses on a charity every year. It has donated money to Habitat for Humanity, which builds homes for those in need. New Avenues for Youth, another charity featured for a few years, has great programs to prevent teen homelessness. The Brewers Fest also bought special equipment for the Oregon Blind Society.

Part of its vision is to make it a family-friendly event. Larrance wanted kids to know that beer isn't bad and to see their parents enjoying a brew responsibly and not binge drinking, which is a more positive view of beer than was previously portrayed. As a bonus, when kids are around, people are calmer, and it cuts down on the craziness.

BREWERS AND BEERS

The Oregon Brew Fest was put together with brewers in mind, not the promoters. The brewers are the stars, and they love to come. They get swag—mugs, tokens, and shirts. There is a Meet the Brewer event where attendees can talk with the brewers and ask them questions.

The festival is a big social gathering for brewers, celebrating the worldwide open-handed brewing community. Many attendees fly into Portland, go to the Brew Fest for a couple days, and spend a day or two touring other local breweries. Larrance wants to highlight the international brewing community, but especially the brewers in the Northwest.

The beers are organized as they arrive. There are two big tents in a five-and-a-half-acre park with thousands of people. The festival has developed a simple system with two serving areas, each with a forty-foot refrigerated trailer and beer lines that run out to coolers with ice. The beers are added to the refrigerated trailer as they arrive. The festival buys sixteen kegs from each brewer and serves more than fifteen hundred kegs of beer.

People can get three-ounce samples of beer for a dollar (there's a line on the mug) or spend four dollars for a full mug.

The organizers work to keep it simple, so a full-time staff doesn't exist. Others have responsibilities, and they communicate online as much as possible, only meeting a few times a year. After the event, there is a follow-up meeting to read reviews and comments from attendees, and Larrance and his team discuss what they can do to make the event better.

There are no food trucks, but five local restaurants come in as vendors, each with one type of food—pizza, burgers, and so on. Why only five? Five ensures that they'll all make a profit. One vendor has returned for each of the thirty-three years.

LEGACY AND THE FUTURE

While it can be beautiful to hold the event outside, it comes with a certain amount of risk. The Brewers Fest is weather sensitive—if it is rainy or too cold, hot, or windy, that can ruin the day. But even when the weather doesn't cooperate, people return, excited for another round of amazing beer.

The Brewers Fest is good for the city as well. Larrance is proud of the economic impact it has on the city, bringing in $20 million a year, and almost half of attendees come from outside of Oregon. A data survey in 2017 concluded that the Brew Fest provided 265 new jobs that year, both directly and indirectly.

Art Larrance has been doing this Brew Fest for three decades, continuing even though he is now in his seventies. He says he keeps doing the event because he's not a quitter. Considering he's someone who helped change the laws of the state, popularized a new industry in Portland, traveled to Europe, and continues to make the Brew Fest better each year, that's easy to believe. In speaking with Larrance, it is easy to catch his passion for craft beer and for the collaborative and friendly craft community not only in Oregon but around the world. He meets new and interesting people every year, and the city of Portland recognizes him.

Oh, and by the way, it's still fun.

What You Need to Know

EVENT Oregon Brewers Festival

WEBSITE https://www.oregonbrewfest.com/

LOCATION Tom McCall Waterfront Park, downtown Portland, Oregon

FOUNDED 1988

DATES Late July

DESIGNATED DRIVER TICKETS AVAILABLE Free admission for everyone

ADMISSION FOR THOSE UNDER TWENTY-ONE Yes

Fifteen-year anniversary glass of the festival.
Photo by Nick Stetina. Courtesy of ICBG, Inc.

CHAPTER FOUR

Festival of Barrel-Aged Beer

Chicago, IL

THE BARREL OF DREAMS

Was it a joke? They couldn't be serious. A beer festival for only barrel-aged beer? That sounded awesome.

While working at the Rock Bottom brewpub in Chicago, Pete Crowley experimented with wood aging his private batches of beer. Bourbon barrels added a deeper flavor. The barrels were readily available from distilleries, since they traditionally used an American white oak barrel only once.

Crowley gathered regularly with his brewer peers at Second City Brewing, sharing his recipes and brews. Other brewers began using barrels to age their beers and innovated with their own aged products.

By 2003, the excitement and interest in barrel-aged beer grew to the point that Crowley organized the first Festival of Barrel-Aged Beer (FoBAB). Twelve breweries brought beer to the festival, held on the second floor of Rock Bottom. Attendees sampled heavy beers with high alcohol by volume (ABV), which lined the outside. Some sampled twice. It became quite a party and paved the way for more growth.

Chicago became known for barrel-aged beer, much as Seattle was known for grunge rock or Los Angeles for 1980s hair metal bands. The city is close to bourbon country, and barrels often travel from Kentucky to Chicago to supply the brewers who continually innovate with the process.

After the first year, FoBAB grew larger, moving from Rock Bottom to the classic Goose Island Brewery. From there it moved to the Chicago Plumbers Union Hall and the Bridgeport Art Center before landing at its current venue—the University of Illinois at Chicago Forum.

The crowded floor of the festival. *Photo by Nick Stetina. Courtesy of ICBG, Inc.*

In 2019, 220 breweries participated—very different from the original twelve. General admission tickets sold out in five minutes when they went on sale in August. No one thought it would expand to its current size.

FIRES AND RIOTS AND BEER

Chicago has an interesting history with beer.

The first brewery in Chicago may have been J&W Crawford's in 1833, but the first to have a real impact was Lill & Diversey Chicago Brewing.[1]

William Haas and Conrad Sulzer initially owned the brewery, but Lill emigrated from England and bought into the brewery, along with William Ogden, the first mayor of Chicago. The money and influence of the mayor, both silent and vocal, helped establish the business in September 1839. When Ogden, Hass, and Sulzer left the company, Michael Diversey came on as a new partner.

Lill & Diversey's Chicago Brewing became one of the biggest beer makers in the West. Their facility ultimately took over an entire city block. Lill's cream ale sold all over the country. The men were generous with their success as well—Diversey regularly donated to German Catholic churches in Chicago.

Seeing success in the industry, other breweries opened over the next three decades. The first lager brewery, also assisted by Mayor Ogden, was John A. Huck's in 1847. J. J. Sands's Columbian Brewery opened in 1855 and rivaled Lill & Diversey's cream ale.[2]

Much of the early brewing in the Midwest began with German immigrants and the German beer culture they brought with them. That German community became the target of anti-immigration movements in the mid-1800s, particularly the Know Nothing Party.

The Know Nothing Movement was a US nativist movement that was anti-Catholic and hostile to immigration. It started as a secret society, so when asked about it in the beginning, members would say they "knew nothing"—hence the name. The movement's platform also included restricting certain kinds of alcohol.

The Know Nothing Party began to win elections and eventually won the mayor's seat in Chicago with Levi Boone in 1855. Targeting the German brewers and German beer culture (immigrants and Catholics), Boone raised the cost of a liquor license 600 percent and began to enforce an old and disregarded ordinance that banned beer sales on Sundays.

German-style beer gardens defied the enforcement of the old law and opened as usual on Sundays. Police entered and arrested the drinkers and threw them in jail—including, in some cases, whole families, as the beer garden was a family social affair. The trial date for these Sunday drinkers approached, and the German neighborhoods protested the abuse of their friends and family. They clashed with police, and both sides fired weapons, injuring several and leading to the Chicago Lager Beer Riots on April 21, 1855.

The conflict ended, and things quieted down by that evening. The riots had several effects. First, Boone backed off his attack on the German beer culture, especially as the German neighborhoods continued to thrive. Second, it discredited the Know Nothing Movement and weakened it for the future.[3]

Third, both the German community and beer became associated with violence, a connection that would later be used during Prohibition.

The Chicago Fire of 1871 was more difficult to fight. The blaze spread and burned over three days in October, destroying 17,500 buildings and killing hundreds.

Five of the twelve Chicago breweries were among those destroyed. Some of the most successful breweries crumbled in a matter of hours—Lill & Diversey, Sands, Brandt, Metz, and Huck.

Beer production slowed to the point that Chicago began importing from nearby Milwaukee, but by 1885, the number of breweries in Chicago had grown to thirty-three. The city became sixth in production of beer and employed two thousand workers at its breweries.

John Seibel, a German immigrant brewer, opened the Siebel Institute of Technology, an organization with the mission of educating professional brewers. Alumni of Siebel oversaw small and large breweries around the world.[4]

Wahl-Henius Institute of Fermentology also opened in the late 1800s.

Along with these influential schools to learn proper brewing, Chicago boasted more than sixty breweries by the early 1900s. In 1891, Peter Hand emigrated from Prussia and opened a brewery that focused on German styles. His Meister Brau became a national drink.

German-style lagers dominate the United States now, but they were new in the mid-1800s, when German immigrants arrived in large numbers. Their entrepreneurial spirit and love of beer culture led them to open several breweries through the Midwest and the United States. The success of this tight-knit community bred resentment among other Americans.

With the rise of the Temperance movement in the United States and with its cultural jealousy of success and the violence of the Chicago Lager Riots in mind, America entered World War I against the "evil" German forces.

Most of the US breweries in the early 1900s were owned by German families—now second- and third-generation Americans—with German names, and they made perfect targets during World War I. These companies were perceived as being owned by the enemy. Added to this, opposition to Prohibition was considered unpatriotic. Those who cared about America wanted to outlaw alcohol, or so the propaganda stated.

The Seibel Institute survived Prohibition by teaching banking. Wahl-Henius Institute of Fermentology didn't make it.[5]

Prohibition, meant to make the nation safer—stopping drunk, abusive husbands and improving the working-class life—did the opposite. It demonized German and Irish immigrants (the drinkers), and the end of the corporate legal structure opened an opportunity for criminal organizations to take over and make tons of money on the black market.

Pouring the barrel-aged brews. *Photo by Nick Stetina. Courtesy of ICBG, Inc.*

These gangs bribed politicians and became territorial, which led to violence. The most famous event was the St. Valentine's Day Massacre in 1929, where a few of Al Capone's men dressed as police officers and gunned down seven men from their rival gang in Chicago.[6]

After Prohibition, Peter Hand Brewery returned and remained, while others shut down or were purchased by the bigger companies that could ride the storm of the Great Depression. Ultimately, the Miller conglomerate bought Hand's Meister Brau, and it became Miller Lite.

The craft brew culture came to Chicago later than to other cities, beginning with Goose Island in 1988. Others followed, such as Two Brothers and Acre Beer Company, but it wasn't until after Metropolitan Brewing opened in 2009 that craft brews surged. With the surge, the common law in many states—where a brewery wasn't allowed to sell its own beer on-site—changed in 2011, and as with many other states, the changing law opened the door to many more craft breweries.[7]

FOUNDED BY THE GUILD

If the Festival of Barrel-Aged Beer is any indication, Chicago isn't hurting anymore.

FoBAB in Chicago is hosted by the Illinois Craft Brewers Guild, a trade association that represents small craft breweries throughout the state. Its mission is to support the development and expansion of the craft beer industry in Illinois.

FoBAB is one of the main fundraisers for the Brewers Guild. It takes place in November in Chicago at the University of Illinois at Chicago's Forum, which has been the venue for the last six years. One of the main draws is the beer competition, which brings in the best of any beer that's touched wood in the aging process.

Most of the breweries are American, although a few international companies have made it to the festival. It is difficult to ship and fly to Chicago, so international participation is minimal.

FoBAB is a unique way to celebrate the natural innovation and ingenuity of the industry and to see what brewers can do with barrel-aged brews. Most brews are porters or strong porters, but others expand into sours and ales or mead. Even ciders are barrel-aged. While the festival is narrow in scope, there is plenty of diversity in styles.

ROLLING ALONG

The setup is organized around eleven or twelve categories as an easy reference for attendees. Signs point people to the bathrooms, always an important aspect of any beer festival.

Since volunteers are trained to pour, the brewers who come can network and interact. They have a good time at the separate VIP brewers lounge, where they receive food and a special dinner the night before the festival kicks off. There is a camaraderie among the brewers. For many of them, the festival is a time to reunite with old friends.

Volunteers help with setup and teardown, and during the event they pour the drinks. Lots of people want to volunteer for FoBAB, since it includes a free ticket to another session. A handful come every year; it's one of their favorite days on the calendar. The consistency and excellence of the volunteers makes it a smooth event and gives it a great vibe.

Getting a picture in front of the barrel wall. *Photo by Nick Stetina.*
Courtesy of ICBG, Inc.

With the fest in the forum, providing food proves to be tricky. There is limited space, so people can buy food at concession areas or leave the forum to eat at one of the local restaurants around the corner. After eating, they can return and continue to enjoy the excellent beers. The festival encourages people to eat beforehand, especially with all the heavy brews that await them.

KNOCK ON WOOD

The venue is a university setting, so the fest reviews the security plan with university staff every year. The security includes off-duty police officers and security provided by the forum. In 2019, the fest's entrance included metal detectors for the first time. The security and volunteers are trained to monitor activity and potential problems throughout the event. They escort people away who may have had too much to drink, which is more likely at a fest with beers so high in ABV.

Fortunately, there have been no major incidents. Knock on wood.

For those who need to get home after the event, the festival suggests ride sharing to and from the forum, which doesn't have much parking. Public transportation is close. A ten-minute cab, Lyft, or Uber ride gets you to the metro, and a bus stop sits just outside the venue on the main intersection of Roosevelt and Halstead. The intersection also provides easy access to cabs, Lyft, and Uber to pick up the attendees.

A big wall with stacks of barrels and lights serves as a backdrop for pics to share with friends.

Different groups come together, including friends from high school or coworkers.

The oasis area on the floor of the forum acts as a getaway from the heavy beers. People can enjoy low-alcohol beers or ciders, sit, and relax. Revolution Brewing sponsored the Oasis area for several years and provided beanbag chairs for participants to use while taking a break from the festival. The setup of the Oasis area depends on the breweries sponsoring it. In 2019, four different breweries sponsored it together and turned it into a campfire experience, complete with lawn chairs, logs, and a fake fire.

People can bring their own water bottles (empty), and they can access water stations that are spread throughout the floor.

FoBAB works with some charities, such as the Sierra Club, the oldest grassroots environmentalist organization in the United States. However, since FoBAB is run by a nonprofit, the Illinois Craft Brewers Guild, it primarily raises funds for that organization.

BARRELS ON TOP

The Chicago Festival of Barrel-Aged Beer opens on Friday night, its first session. The next session is on Saturday afternoon and includes announcements of the winners of the festival competition in each category. That is the most popular session with brewers and attendees. The fest ends Saturday night, often with an after party at a local Chicago brewery.

Brewers love to enter the competition. There are gold, silver, and bronze medals in each of a dozen categories. The top prizes are the Best in Show and the runner-up. The competition remains a foundational aspect of the festival and led to much of its growth.

The judges for the competition aren't novices. They have extensive prior experience in judging and are vetted down to one hundred people. The FoBAB team works together to make the competition fair and the judges the best they can find. Judging begins on Friday morning and continues into the afternoon before the event begins.

The awards are prestigious. Watching the joy and victory on the faces of brewers shows the importance of the hard work and value of innovation. Once the winners are announced on Saturday afternoon, people explore and sample the award-winning beers during the session on Saturday evening.

AGED TO PERFECTION

FoBAB attendees love the unique beers they can sample, beers they wouldn't have access to anywhere else since most of the brewers are local to their own regions. Breweries also get creative, and the attendees can access beers that might not even make it to market.

Craft beer is a people's movement. It began with individuals using make-shift equipment to brew beer in their kitchens, garages, basements, or living

The beauty of the barrel
Photo by Nick Stetina. Courtesy of ICBG, Inc.

Programs and the commemorative glass. *Photo by Nick Stetina. Courtesy of ICBG, Inc.*

rooms. Sharing recipes and experimenting with brews led to a community where people feel connected. It is by people for people—for friends.

The primary motivation of the craft community is great beer, not money, marketing, or corporate takeovers. The craft beer culture is resistant, at its heart, to all those things.

A culture of creativity, raising the bar, and empowerment makes it a great family to be a part of.

The Chicago Festival of Barrel-Aged beer is a prime example of this. Pete Crowley began with making private batches in his home, sharing them with friends, and loving the taste of the beer he aged in white oak barrels. It was natural to share what he loved with like-minded others in a festival.

It started small, and Pete is no longer running the Illinois Craft Brewers Guild. People such as current executive director Danielle D'Allesandro have kept the love of craft beer and the heart of FoBAB alive as it has grown, expanding in Illinois and around the country, farther than people dreamed.

Dreams can look like jokes at first, but those dreams can catch on. A festival of wood-aged beer that started with twelve breweries now has 220 and sells out in minutes, months before the event. Not a joke at all. It really happened.

What You Need to Know

EVENT Festival of Barrel-Aged Beer

WEBSITE https://fobab.com/

LOCATION UIC Forum, 725 W. Roosevelt Rd., Chicago, IL

FOUNDED 2003

DATES Mid-November

DESIGNATED DRIVER TICKETS AVAILABLE No

ADMISSION FOR THOSE UNDER TWENTY-ONE
  Infants worn in carriers

Commemorative Brewgaloo Festival glass.
Courtesy of Shop Local Raleigh.

CHAPTER FIVE

Brewgaloo Beer Fest

Raleigh, NC

RESILIENT

Jennifer Martin didn't know whether she'd have a job the next day.

Brewgaloo Beer Fest is an outdoor festival, and in the third year of the growing event, rain poured for eight hours, keeping the crowd low and attendance down.

Martin is a pro, and she had rain insurance. However, precipitation was measured at the airport, twenty minutes away. Unfortunately, the level was a tenth of an inch lower than what she needed to claim the insurance.

The organization that hosts the event as one of their main fundraisers, Shop Local Raleigh, lost $25,000 that day.

Martin kept her job and worked like crazy over the summer with other fundraising events to make up the loss. The next year, Brewgaloo did raise money, and within eighteen months, Martin and Shop Local Raleigh made all the money back.

It would have been easy to give up. But Martin believed in the event and in the cause—highlighting North Carolina craft breweries and raising money for Shop Local Raleigh, which supports and encourages local businesses.

Like many beer fests, the Brewgaloo is a passion project. Yes, it's about beer, but the passion extends to local businesses and the community.

COMMUNITY BREWS

Back in 2011, Martin and Shop Local Raleigh began hearing from local craft breweries in the community. Many went to the major beer fests on a donation model. In this model, the brewery brings its own beer in the hopes that

Packed crowds in downtown Raleigh. *Courtesy of Shop Local Raleigh.*

attendees will sample it, become fans, and come to the brewery. Often the breweries don't get those fans—distance and local interest are factors—and then they lose money. Craft breweries are local companies without the margins to lose money like that.

At the same time, food trucks were becoming more popular. The combination of rise in local breweries and food truck popularity gave Jennifer Martin ideas.

Shop Local Raleigh has a stated mission: "Promoting and supporting locally-owned, independent businesses. It's about making your hard-earned money go further, fueling the local economy, and helping to preserve the unique character of Raleigh." The culture of local craft breweries fits well with the organization, making it the perfect type of business to support.

Martin asked the breweries, "What if there was a festival where the event paid for the beer? Would that solve the problem?" The breweries said yes.

Then the questions began. Where should they hold the festival? If they had it at one large brewery, then two problems arose. First, it would be limited to that space. Second, the festival would promote that brewery more than the others. In addition, a large brewery might not be centrally located.

Martin wanted to make it affordable as well. Many of the beer fests charged high admission costs. She also didn't want to compete with the other festivals. How could they be unique?

They made attendance free and charged people only for what they drank (by pint and sample) and controlled their expenses.

Martin chose Downtown Raleigh for the event space. They would block off the entire downtown area and take it over.

The guiding principle of the festival is local. All beer is North Carolina beer on tap. The breweries must be owned and headquartered in the state; they cannot be second locations or owned from out-of-state companies.

The food trucks, bands, and vendors are all from the Triangle region of North Carolina. The Triangle is the area between Raleigh, Durham, and Chapel Hill. It's also the area between University of North Carolina, Duke, and North Carolina State, and it was named after Research Triangle Park.

In the first year, Shop Local hoped that fifteen hundred people would attend. Forty-five hundred showed up. The next year it grew to ten thousand, and then thirty thousand. In 2019, sixty thousand people attended. Brewgaloo is one of the largest beer fests in the country, run by a staff of two, and it won the Best Beer Fest in America by *USA Today* in 2019.

FROM HOUSEWIVES TO MICROBREWS

Before European colonists arrived, Native Americans made beer from cedar berries and corn or possibly molasses.

The first English colonists in 1585 founded Roanoke Colony, and beer was a mainstay of their diets. Homemakers brewed the drink in their private homes, although taverns served local or country beer, with some English imports. Other imports came from New York or Philadelphia.

As the colony grew, brewing diminished. Transportation to rural areas was poor. Farmers discovered that it was easier to turn their extra grain into whiskey, which kept better and took up less room. They could also carry it in little flasks for ease.

Antebellum North Carolina restricted African Americans from consuming or selling alcohol, and during the Civil War, the state outlawed brewing altogether.[1] Temperance painted a dark picture where alcohol was responsible for all of society's ills—crime, poverty, disease, and orphaned children. Prohibition came early to the state, since the counties had the option of being "dry" or not. Sixty-eight counties voted to ban alcohol in 1881. North

Long look down the street during the festival. *Courtesy of Shop Local Raleigh.*

Carolina became the first state to adopt Prohibition by direct vote in 1908. Even when Prohibition was federally repealed, counties still retained the option, and much of the state remained dry. North Carolina was one of two states to vote against the repeal.

The repeal happened in 1933, and in 1937, North Carolina passed the Alcoholic Beverage Control Bill, which placed huge restrictions on alcohol, notably the amount of alcohol brewed and sold in the state and a cap on the alcohol by volume (ABV) level of 6 percent. Brewpubs (which produced and sold on the same site) were also illegal.

Consumption of alcohol didn't rise in the state until after World War II. More communities allowed beer, more people with a different attitude toward alcohol migrated to the state, beer advertising increased, and incomes rose now that the nation was out of the war and Depression.

The first breweries in the state were larger companies, notably Strohs, Schlitz, and later Miller.[2]

When mircrobrewing increased around the country in the 1980s and 1990s, North Carolina saw the success of small, local establishments, which increased demand for darker, heavier English ales, hailing back to the colonial brewing traditions of centuries earlier.

First the brewpub law was repealed in 1985 through a lobbying campaign by Uli Benniwitz. Benniwitz also opened North Carolina's first brewpub in 1985, the Weeping Radish.

The first brewery in the bursting city of Asheville opened in 1994. Oscar Wong and John McDermott founded the Highland Brewing Company. Their flagship Gaelic Ale was popular around the Southeast.

Despite interest and mountainous regions that were perfect for highland stream water in a great craft brew, North Carolina craft breweries lagged behind the rest of the country for one specific reason—the 6 percent ABV cap. They couldn't brew certain styles of beer or experiment above that limit, hampering production and diversification at the taps.

Music and brews. *Courtesy of Shop Local Raleigh.*

Sean Wilson of Fullsteam Brewery led the Pop the Cap movement. Wilson is known as North Carolina's top spokesperson for local craft breweries. After two years of work and lobbying with other owners of breweries in the state, the cap was raised from 6 percent to 15 percent, opening the door for breweries to experiment with new styles.

Just like Martin overcame the setback of year three of the Brewgaloo to have one of the top beer fests in the country, North Carolina boasts a thriving craft culture. There are now over three hundred breweries and brewpubs in the state, the most in the South. Last year, North Carolina breweries brought home twelve medals from the Great American Beer Fest.[3]

SET UP AND CELEBRATE

The main event for Brewgaloo is from 2:00 p.m. to 10:00 p.m. on the fourth Saturday of April, but Friday night is an opportunity for a more intimate setting, the Block Party.

For the Friday Night Block Party, Shop Local Raleigh shuts down one block downtown. People can purchase entry tickets and receive cups to sample from thirty-five breweries at their leisure. There is a DJ instead of a band and only a few vendors. The Block Party gives the beer connoisseur who doesn't like crowds a way to enjoy great beer and talk to the brewers.

The Block Party was added on year five of the Brewgaloo and has become wildly popular. Eight hundred tickets are sold, and these sell out quickly every year.

Being on a city street makes setup and teardown a tricky endeavor. There is only a limited time to shut the street down, and workers must get in and out fast. The Friday Block Party has the added benefit of extra time to set up the night before. The block is shut down from 6:00 p.m. to 10:00 p.m. on Friday. At 10:00 p.m., workers clean up and get ready for the next day.

At 11:00 p.m., Brewgaloo has access to the rest of the street. The tent company begins lining the street with tents and works until 2:00 or 3:00 a.m. Portable toilets and barricades are loaded in along with the tents.

Workers and volunteers come back at 6:00 a.m. on Saturday to bring in the vendors. A map of the layout is prepared in advance (on Thursday) as a reference for vendors, breweries, and food trucks, and everyone is given their section to set up. In the eighth year, the system works like a machine. Breweries enter from one end of the street to load. Everything happens before the opening at 2:00 p.m. The governor kicks off the event every year.

Dance party. *Courtesy of Shop Local Raleigh.*

At 10:00 p.m., the festival shuts down, and everyone works to break down everything to be out by 4:00 a.m. They must have it looking exactly like it did before.

Each brewery gets a ten-by-ten-foot space for its booth. Food trucks have bigger areas. One side of the street is for ticketing only. Attendees walk through three main entrances where they are IDed, get a plastic mug, and buy beer tickets.

GETTING ON THE STREET

During the first few years, Brewgaloo tried other methods for beer trade-ins, from wooden tokens to coins. They found that carnival-style tickets worked the best. They sell two tickets for one dollar, and people buy them from the ticketing stations.

There is an online option to register (again, for free), but about half of the people register on-site.

Because it is on a city street, everyone is welcome to Brewgaloo. Dads with strollers can be seen. When the night rolls around, fewer kids are in attendance.

Rocking the brew crowd. *Courtesy of Shop Local Raleigh.*

Fifty food trucks are spaced throughout the downtown street. An application process ensures a good variety of different kinds of food and desserts. The most popular trucks are BBQ, and it is a challenge to rotate them around and space them out. Brewgaloo is loyal to the food trucks that have been on board with them since year one. They took a chance on this crazy, new festival. Would it be successful? They were rewarded for their risk with a profitable event.

EVERYONE WELCOME AND SAFE

Brewgaloo wants to be kid and family friendly, and they have a zero-tolerance policy for anyone who gets out of control. They call taxis or rides to get people out and home safe. Brewgaloo doesn't want it to be a drunk festival, and they take responsibility for being proactive and making sure everyone is safe.

Security is a combination of off-duty officers and a staffing company. The local company helps check IDs at the gates and has someone at every entry and exit point. The volunteers and staff, along with the breweries and food trucks, are trained to be the eyes and ears, calling about any incidents immediately.

The festival works with a local taxi company, 919, reserving a special area for them with easy access for those who need it.

Since Shop Local Raleigh is nonprofit and this is one of their main fundraisers for the year, they pull in everyone from their board of directors and other members of the organization to volunteer and get involved in some way, whether setting up, cleaning up, or working a booth. Then Brewgaloo sends out a call to the public.

Volunteers at the first shifts get free tickets for the later one. In one year, there was an after party for all of the volunteers, but free tickets for beer proved to be the best motivators. The fest attempted an after party at a go cart or other entertainment venue for the last shift, but with the night getting late and the volunteers exhausted, they found it easier to give gift cards or passes for entertainment options on another day.

Other nonprofits have opportunities to volunteer also, in exchange for donations to their organizations.

The main cleanup involves the tents and other structures. Volunteers don't clean the trash on the street. A separate company is hired to make sure it is pristine for Sunday morning.

QUITE A HOBBY

When Brewgaloo first began, it had a staff of one, Jennifer Martin, who runs the Shop Local, an organization similar to a small chamber of commerce, with 850 members. They promote businesses on social media, offer mentoring and networking, and teach seminars, all to help grow local businesses.

The festival wasn't that profitable in the beginning. Martin called it her hobby. She worked at Shop Local by day and Brewgaloo at night. It was a labor of love for the cause of local businesses.

Brewgaloo has grown. Now there's a staff of two.

A core group of eight volunteers exists, however, and their input is invaluable. They come to every planning meeting to share ideas and insight and make sure Brewgaloo improves each year.

Martin is proud that local businesses have become more successful.

When one brewery came to its first Brewgaloo, it was small and wasn't distributing. The wait at the sample line at the festival became an hour long, and their beers are now among the most popular. People can find their beers on shelves in stores today.

Other breweries come out before they even open just to sell merchandise and T-shirts. They use the festival to get exposure and talk to people. Brewgaloo doesn't charge those breweries to have a booth, and when the brewery does open, they have an email list of fans who are ready to try their beers.

Other businesses share in the success as well. Some food trucks started with Brewgaloo and grew their businesses. Some vendors began as pop-ups and now have brick-and-mortar shops.

FUN EVERYWHERE YOU LOOK

There are two main music stages, one at each end of the street. The first is on the steps of the state capital; the second is at the city plaza downtown. In the middle, they used to have acoustic acts in front of the courthouse, but then they switched to a DJ—easier to set up—which has become its own dance party.

One year, the Stanley Cup trophy came to the festival, and they worked with the local NHL teams to come create a fan zone. People got to take pictures with the cup.

Brewgaloo added a fourth stage with acapella acts. Recently, a young man who plays the violin performed. He had become famous on *America's Got Talent.*

People can sit on the green in the beer garden area, listen to music, and hang out.

Local businesses have the option of reserving an area with tent space to meet with staff or friends.

The local Harley dealership brought in a simulator ride—a mechanical platform where people could sit on a Harley motorcycle and pretend they were riding along mountain roads. It was a very popular attraction.

A local tennis academy brought out a smaller tennis court where people played tennis matches. One year, the festival provided electric bikes to ride through the event and side plazas. There are games like giant Jenga and ring toss.

IT'S ABOUT THE BEER

But the beer is the main attraction.

There aren't any homebrew competitions due to the alcohol laws in North Carolina. Special beers are made for the event, but they don't have competitions for the brewers either. The motto is to keep it simple and highlight all the North Carolina breweries and craft beers.

Party into the night. *Courtesy of Shop Local Raleigh.*

Over one hundred portable toilets are spaced throughout the event, and there are handwashing stations. The festival also reminds attendees that local businesses aren't for bathroom purposes. Food trucks sell water bottles, and big water towers, which hold the equivalent of one thousand water bottles, are available to fill beer mugs when needed.

While the Brewgaloo already brings immense value to the community, they have plans to be more generous in the future. They want to provide scholarships or equipment for the brewing lab at a nearby college with a brewing program. Shop Local will include space to start and help new businesses in the new building that is now under construction.

Attendees love that it is dog and pet friendly. They appreciate the environment downtown and the rare ability to drink openly in the streets. The event is not cost prohibitive. Other events are expensive and difficult for people to get their money's worth. The long time span allows people to come and go as they please.

Of course, attendees also love the beers. The ability to sample local breweries and beers from all over North Carolina brings people back every year.

The first few years involved constant growth and adding more space. Year one filled one downtown block. Year two filled two blocks, and year three filled four. They met their five-year plan in three years.

The Brewgaloo is now maxed out in size with 150 breweries with two to six taps each, which represents a vast and diverse selection. Now they focus on how to make it better. How do they perfect it? They've been hiring more people for the entry lines to shorten wait times. They've streamlined the online process. The beer purchasing was fine-tuned to prevent wasting so much beer at the end of the festival. Waste cuts into the profit and fundraising. Adjustments to little things made every year keep it relevant and improving.

VALUE BEYOND ONE DAY

At the end of the day, the event is a partnership with the city, local businesses, vendors, food trucks, breweries, volunteers, and security. Everyone needs to be on their A game. Martin couldn't do it without every group's participation and passion, working together to help support each other for new and sustainable businesses.

The Brewgaloo continues to have residual effects in growing small businesses and celebrating the importance of craft beer in North Carolina.

The local community is a huge aspect of what makes craft breweries so attractive. The ability to meet the brewmaster, give feedback, slow down and have a treasure of high-quality beverages in your backyard—all of it connects to the power and interest in loyalty to local business.

That passion for community drives Martin and Shop Local Raleigh to continue to put on one of the largest award-winning beer fests in the country. She doesn't have to worry about her job much these days.

What You Need to Know

EVENT Brewgaloo Beer Fest

WEBSITE https://shoplocalraleigh.org/brewgaloo/

LOCATION Downtown Raleigh, NC

FOUNDED 2011

DATES Fourth weekend in April

DESIGNATED DRIVER TICKETS AVAILABLE Free admission for all

ADMISSION FOR THOSE UNDER TWENTY-ONE No for the Friday
  Night Block Party; yes for the Saturday Street Fest

CHAPTER SIX

Great Taste of the Midwest

Madison, WI

THE PREGAME

The party begins on Friday night, spreading all over Madison, Wisconsin, and leads up to the festival. Friday night is known as Great Taste Eve.

Local craft breweries in the city work with breweries, restaurants, taverns, beer bars, and other establishments to set up special events at different venues. There are beer pairing dinners, which combine great food with craft beer. Breweries go head-to-head in friendly competitions, or breweries from one state square off against another. More than sixty different events are spread throughout the whole city.

Great Taste Eve has become a big deal, especially for out-of-towners who have something to do the night before the Great Taste of the Midwest festival and for breweries that have come in from out of town and developed relationships over the years.

It's a tradition in the city of Madison, the capital of Wisconsin and the home of the University of Wisconsin. Part capital, part college town, it's the perfect spot for a beer fest.

The Great Taste of the Midwest is the nation's second-longest-running beer fest; only the Great American Beer Fest is older.

The foundation of the festival is homebrewers gone wild. As homebrewers in the state started discovering beer that they liked to drink in the late 1970s and 1980s, they traveled to places such as Europe and loved the flavors and styles they couldn't get in the United States.

Then a member of the Homebrew Club visited the first Great American Beer Fest in Boulder, Colorado, and was impressed with the craft brew

Get ready to enter the park for the festival.
Photo by and courtesy of Scott Maurer.

Music in the park. *Photo by and courtesy of Scott Maurer.*

culture and the exposure to new styles and beers. Could they do something like that in Madison?

Three years later, they did just that. They reached out to twenty-five breweries from the Midwest and gathered at the Italian Working Men's Club in Madison for the first Great Taste of the Midwest. It was something no one else had experienced—except for Bob Drousth, that is, whose claim to fame is that he attended both the first Great American and the first Great Taste festivals.

Some breweries, such as Capital Brewery, which opened in 1986, have been to the first Great Taste of the Midwest festival and to every one since. On the second Saturday in August, the Great Taste moved outdoors into parks and, in 1997, moved to Olin Park, the "crown jewel" of the Madison park system. Surrounded by century-old trees on a hillside next to Lake Monoma, the park has a view of the capital building and the downtown skyline. It's a picturesque setting with an amazing feel for the festival.

BEER CAPITAL OF THE WORLD

Wisconsin is the perfect state for a beer fest. It was the home of the beer revolution in the 1800s.

In colonial America, alcohol remained a necessity of daily life. The idea of moderation dominated the philosophy. Alcohol was good, as long as it didn't interfere with worship and work.

But beer took time and care, and it was difficult to preserve. As the country grew west, pioneers and hardworking Americans couldn't waste time on barley or hops. Cider and brandy proved easier to produce, and rum was cheap.[1]

Americans drank to get the buzz, guzzling with no thought of social pleasure or community, which created problems. Along with the early Puritan religious influence, people in the United States no longer saw alcohol as a necessity but as a problem.

In this context, immigration boomed in the mid-1800s. There were six hundred thousand immigrants in the 1830s, 1.7 million in the 1840s, and 2.6 million in the 1850s. Three-quarters of them were from Germany and Ireland.

Beer drinkers.

The Irish had a drinking culture, but they were fleeing the potato famine and abject poverty in their own country. The desperate and poor Irish were just trying to survive.

The Germans left their country due to riots, famine, and land disputes. There was political oppression, and young men looking for the promise of opportunity left for America. They were independent minded entrepreneurs. While the Irish stayed on the east coast, the Germans made their way into the Midwest, bringing their culture and brewing craft with them.[2]

Brewing had been part of German culture for centuries, and German people brought that culture with them when they came to America. Small breweries soon dotted the landscape in the United States. In many small towns, breweries were the first businesses, built in residential locations. Brewing alcohol was a local thing. Most breweries didn't last more than a few years, but a select few ambitious business owners thrived while making great beer.

Legendary brewer Philip Best began his brewery, Philip Best Brewing, in 1841, and it became the nation's largest in 1874. They made cheese during Prohibition, became Pabst, and then bought headquarters in Los Angeles, where they moved.

Originally the August Krug Brewery, Joseph Schlitz Brewing opened in 1849, and Schlitz became the nation's largest in 1902. It became known as the beer that made Milwaukee famous.

Valentin Blatz Brewing came in 1851 and was the first company to bottle beer in 1874. Now they are owned by Miller.

The year 1855 saw the start of Miller Brewing. It was originally Plank Road Brewing, made the first lite beer in the twentieth century, and was bought out by larger interests.

A few factors worked together to help these companies become wildly successful.

In the United States, English ale was never as popular as cider and spirits. German immigrants introduced the lager, which was light in body and color and had a lower alcoholic content. The rising German population and curious American drinkers who were ready for something lighter created demand.

Most breweries didn't survive because their towns didn't have the populations to keep them going. For Pabst, Miller, Blatz and others, the small population meant they had to figure out how to expand and distribute. It forced them to think on a national scale and develop long-distance shipping.

Milwaukee was close to big Chicago, with beer drinkers and German culture galore. The Chicago Fire in 1871 gave Milwaukee breweries a huge boost.[3]

Men such as Philip Best and Joseph Schlitz ensured the quality of the beer was paramount. They thought creatively and were willing to adapt and use new technology. Breweries built icehouses and took advantage of advances in pasteurization and transportation (railroad, etc.)

Combine all those factors with the fresh water of the Milwaukee River, cold winters with ice to keep beer cold and fresh, and deep caves to store barrels in, and it led to Milwaukee becoming the home of American brewing, the beer capital of the world.[4]

These German immigrants re-created their culture of social pleasure, connected with great beer, and adapted it for America. Americans latched onto German lager as social drinking and a compromise between the extremes of Temperance and gluttonous drinking. The German culture flew in the face of the Temperance message. Here was a culture that proved it was possible to combine alcohol with respectability, industry, pleasure, and decency.[5]

Competition leads to crazy booths. *Photo by and courtesy of Scott Maurer.*

One of the American adaptations of the German culture, however, was big, competitive business. It wasn't only about being successful but about crushing the competition. The big brewers began to crush the smaller ones.

At the same time, the German and Irish drinking culture clashed with the American hate for alcohol. Combined with anti-immigrant feelings, the fight with Germany in World War I, and legitimate problems with several American saloons that used illegal activities to stay alive as big breweries fought for dominance, Prohibition passed.

Prohibition laws achieved the opposite of their intent, increasing the crime, corruption, and chaos they were meant to stop.

Wisconsin had 165 breweries before Prohibition. When the law was repealed in the early 1930s, eighty-eight were left. Over the next few decades, the big brewing companies took over more of the market, and by the 1970s, only eight remained in the state.

Craft beer came to the rescue. The local, collaborative focus of craft brew came to the state like it did to others—with homebrewers, and then the opening of microbreweries and brewpubs around the state. In the shadow of the brewing giants, places such as New Glarus in Middleton and others in Milwaukee and in small towns popped up around the state.

The resurgence of craft brewing in the last decade included Port Huron Brewing Company in 2012, the first in Columbia County since Eulbery Brewery closed in 1958. Port Huron brewmaster, Tanner Brethorst, had a dream. He studied brewing at the famous Siebel Institute in Chicago and improved his methods under other Wisconsin brewers.[6]

Now Wisconsin has about 130 breweries. That growth has only improved the experience of the Great Taste of the Midwest.

THE TRADITION AND INNOVATION OF THE MIDWEST

The Great Taste only serves beers from the Midwest. It features eleven states from the Dakotas to Kansas, Kentucky, and Ohio and everything in between. In 2019, beautiful Olin Park saw two hundred breweries with fourteen hundred beers and ten thousand attendees for the event.

The festival requires breweries to staff and support their own tables. The brewers and owners pour and discuss their brews and where they are from. Great Taste has developed knowledgeable fans who want that access to ask educated questions: How was the beer made? What did you dry hop with? What is the brew system?

This way, the attendee is more connected with the glass, and it is close to the tap-room experience at a local brewery, except at a large festival.

It's about the beer. Each brewery brings a minimum of six or seven brews. Others bring more. Dark Horse from Marshall, Michigan, brought thirty beers on the thirtieth anniversary of the festival. Great Dane, based in Madison, brought a record thirty-seven beers one year.

Breweries that have been with Great Taste for a long time bring loads of beer. They want to make it fun and showcase their selection. Some breweries bring verticals, such as a barrel-aged series from the current year and from several years prior to compare and show how beers and recipes evolve through three to five beers in the same line. Attendees list this as a great feature and wait in long lines to participate.

Most of the breweries are in large tents, twenty-five to thirty under one roof. Patrons line up outside the tent and are served once they enter. The bigger breweries or those that bring several beers have their own tents to accommodate the longer lines. Those tables tend to be more elaborate.

Bluegrass at the festival. *Photo by and courtesy of Scott Maurer.*

Pours are two-ounce samples. People want the variety and ability to taste several beers and be selective about them. Because the fest is in the park, people can dump the beer on the ground if they don't like it, which is a nice feature.

SETUP AND ORGANIZATION

As the event is in August, hydration is a serious issue. Water stations are situated throughout the park for people to fill either water bottles they bring or the sample glasses. People can drink the water from the rinsing stations in multiple locations. After rinsing and drinking, people go back for more beer.

The festival has seventy-five staff, but 650 volunteers run the event. There is little turnover for the volunteer positions, and many have served since the early years. They are passionate and helpful. The volunteers feel like a part of the festival, even if they aren't members of the Homebrew Club or on staff. They express excitement and contribute willingly to make the day better.

The Great Taste of the Midwest is on the second Saturday in August, from 1:00 p.m. to 6:00 p.m. All tickets sales are online; there are no on-site ticket sales. The festival starts setting up in Olin Park on Thursday. On Friday, setup wraps up, and the beer deliveries begin.

The park has a permanent bathroom facility, but the festival spreads around another 130 portable toilets. That's almost one portable toilet per brewery!

The Madison Police Department helps with security, both inside the event and outside for traffic flow. A private security firm is also hired to assist with details on that day.

Sampling the brews. *Photo by and courtesy of Scott Maurer.*

The Great Taste takes avoiding drinking and driving seriously. It is a nondriving event. The festival takes up the parking lots, so people can't drive to it and park there. It provides shuttles to eleven different stops and breweries, brewpubs, bars, and other places. Great Taste also subsidizes cab rides. People can get a cab for one dollar, available to all patrons, and pickup is right at the park. The line forms on the soccer field just outside the festival grounds, and there is a long line of cabs—basically a whole local taxi company. The one-dollar cab rides make staying safe an easy decision. Generous tips are encouraged!

The food at the festival is great. There are food trucks and catering options with tents and tables. All food vendors are local, and there is everything from Jamaican food, subs, pizza, Mediterranean, tacos, BBQ, falafel, and more.

Wherever people are, they aren't far from beer, water, or food.

ENTERTAINMENT

Or music.

There are twenty different musical acts in the park at one time. There is no stage, and it's informal. Musicians donate their time and talent. They come into the festival, find a tree with some shade, set up, and start playing. There are string quartets, washboard and banjo bands, bluegrass, and folk. There was even a New Orleans style horn section once that wound its way through the crowd, conga style, picking up people along the way to join in. People never know what musical treats they will hear.

The only festival competition is for table design. This competition celebrates creativity in the decoration of each brewer's table or booth. A team of judges roams through the grounds and awards the best table design.

As one can imagine, the booths get crazy.

One year, a brewery set up a whole Blues Brothers theme, complete with a stage wrapped in chicken wire and a live band playing blues music. An old police car painted like the Blues mobile, with a loudspeaker on the roof, was parked nearby. Other booths had a maze of bourbon barrels to get to the beers, bars made out of boats, firetrucks, vintage airstreams, and converted RVs.

One year, a brewery went to the college dorms and apartments around town when students were moving in and out. They collected old couches that were being thrown out, set six out on the grass, and called it the couch party.

CHARITIES AND COMPETITIONS

The Homebrew Club is already a nonprofit, so they aren't lining their pockets with money from the festival. Great Taste takes pride in raising money for local charities.

WORT, the local public access radio station in Madison, supported the festival early on. They sent volunteers. Great Taste donated money back to the radio station, and as local radio has declined, it's been even more important for the festival to give money back to the station.

The Homebrew Club holds its meetings through the year at the Wil-Mar Community Center in Madison. This neighborhood community center is in a 120-year-old church and requires renovations to modernize and repair it. The Great Taste has donated significant funds for the renovation in addition to the rent and other donations through the year.

The festival donates to summer camps for kids with autism, domestic violence shelters, youth groups, and other community charities that need funding to keep the lights on.

An interesting charity is the Ice Age Trail, working for land procurement and trail maintenance over fifteen hundred miles through the Midwest. The Ice Age Trail marks glacier migration.

The festival started with a love of beer, wanting to expose people to the craft beer that the homebrewers loved, and it grew with "beer geeks" in mind—aficionados of brewing and malts and hops and flavors.

Part of the festival is the "conversion," turning people on to a new beer or beer in general. Often, people think they don't like beer, but it's really bad beer that they don't like. Given a taste of a great brew, many people realize that they love beer.

Jason Walters has been with the festival for over fifteen years, and his mother attended for the first time in 2019. She was not a beer drinker, but within thirty minutes, she was smiling with a brew in her hand and said, "I found a beer I really like!" It was a coffee stout, not what one would expect for a first beer. Since she was a coffee drinker, it was a perfect fit for her.

THE BEST OF THE MIDWEST

What do people say they love about the Great Taste? Depends on who is asked.

Brewers give the biggest compliments. They are blown away with the execution and logistics and how they are treated—like rock stars. Since they feel so appreciated, they work hard to make a good impression and bring special beers, some released just for the festival. The patrons benefit from those connections and efforts.

The attendees love having access to "unicorn beers" they could never get on their own. The beer geeks write notes and give reviews on the app Untappd. They wait in line for specific beers they want to try that are only available on that day. The geeks get jazzed about the beers that blow their minds with flavor and unique combinations. The casual fan spends a beautiful day in a beautiful park with great people, having a great time with food and fun music.

It's the ultimate party. It's not about guzzling beer but about experiencing quality in the community. It's a party where everyone feels safe, has fun, and wants to come back next year to party again.

What You Need to Know

EVENT   Great Taste of the Midwest

WEBSITE   https://greattaste.org/

LOCATION   Olin Park, Madison, WI

FOUNDED   1987

DATES   Second Saturday in August

DESIGNATED DRIVER TICKETS AVAILABLE   Yes

ADMISSION FOR THOSE UNDER TWENTY-ONE
   Admission is free for those under sixteen, as well as those
   with a designated driver ticket

CHAPTER SEVEN

Culmination Beer Fest

Anchorage, AK

THE PEOPLE'S MOVEMENT

One of the marvels of the modern craft beer industry is the departure in mindset from the corporate giants and their competition for domination that marked the late 1800s. Pabst, Miller, Busch, and others survived the epic periods of Prohibition, the Great Depression, and World War II, but great taste and quality were sacrificed for the new American consumer who wanted things cheap and convenient.

Young men and women through the 1970s rebelled against such notions, not just in beer but in life. With beer, however, it expressed itself in a very different but still American way. The individualism and empowerment remained; the industriousness and hard work never left. In the desire to have beer that tasted amazing with great quality, homebrewers entered the scene. Many adjusted and worked hard to become professional. Many failed, and some didn't.

As was already stated, craft brewing became a people's movement, the best of what America has to offer in its culture, creativity, and inclusion. It is not a pyramid scheme but a grassroots movement, the desire to see every major town have a brewery.

Beer fests also sprung from that movement. Even the biggest of them endeavor for those aspects of the craft brew movement.

Part of the appeal of the movement is the intimate, personal connection between the brewer, the beer, and the drinker. It's something heard in all conversations or interviews.

One of the people who see that connection as integral is Gabe Fletcher.

Fletcher was born in Vermont but grew up in the wonderful environment of Alaska. He ran a local brewery in Alaska, Midnight Sun, for thirteen years before opening his own, Anchorage Brewing, in 2010.

Connected with the local craft scene for over twenty years, he also had an appreciation for the national community. Because of the distance and isolation, beer fests in Alaska focused on state breweries, which were few, but they were famous for their bold brews. With that appreciation for the local community, he was also concerned that people in Anchorage (or the state) weren't connected with the breweries in the rest of the United States.

He decided to start an Alaskan beer fest that highlighted US beers and his continental friends in the industry. It was important to his vision that the festival be small and intimate—no more than 350 people. Fletcher would pay for the beer, ship it, fly in the brewers, and bring in good food for one hundred dollars a person.

At most festivals, people drink and eat before and after the festival—drinking all night at times. Fletcher enjoyed activities such as hiking and fishing and sought to incorporate the Alaskan outdoors into the festival as a way for brewers to relax and enjoy themselves.

THE THREE Bs

Craft beer has been growing in Alaska over the last couple of decades, but beer first grew as an industry during the Gold Rush of the mid-1800s. Thousands of prospectors came to find gold, and brewers soon followed to quench their thirst. Beer also provided safer drinking water than the local options.

Those first breweries were technically illegal. The United States bought Alaska from Russia in March 1867 and turned it into a Native American territory where alcohol wasn't legal. The rare federal agents who operated in Alaska ignored the brewing, however, especially when they were enjoying the brews themselves.

The first breweries were in Sitka in 1874 and Juneau in 1886. Those two breweries succeeded as settlers came into the territory, but they didn't survive long past the early twentieth century.

Skagway became famous for a lot of things, one of them being its breweries. The saloons began as dirty, desperate tent operations (all the local establishments were tents at first), but the Gold Rush brought in more people and money, and those saloons moved into stand-alone buildings.

The 1899 state law legalized drinking establishments, opening the door for local breweries to pop up with more modern equipment, selling the beer to those saloons.

The economy crashed as quickly as the Gold Rush boomed, and due to the combination of competition from Seattle breweries and a growing Temperance campaign by the wives of local community leaders, brewing in Skagway became difficult. The breweries and business owners pursued the miners going north, leading to a pattern of short success and failure, as those communities grew and waned.

In the years between 1880 and 1918, every town had a brewery. Temporary settlements abounded, and the running joke was that a trading post would soon be its own town if it had the three Bs—a bakery, brewery, and brothel.

Prohibition closed many breweries, but even when the law was repealed, concerns about World War II (Alaska was closer to the Soviet Union, Japan, and the war than people realize) and the subsequent fight for statehood in 1959 kept brewing low on the list of priorities. The national standard continued to be cheap beer by big giants, so the demand for anything local or higher quality didn't exist.

Until the 1970s, that is, when German investors convinced the state to subsidize a new local brewery in Alaska, the "Last Frontier." Prinz Brau opened in 1976 with great fanfare and saturated marketing, but there were several problems—a grasshopper infestation in the barley supply, controversy and legal problems over the nonunionized workers at the brewery, and the popularity of other national brands. The biggest hit on Prinz Brau was its thin and tepid lager. It didn't taste very good, and as any brewer will tell you, the beer must taste great.

Prinz Brau went belly-up in 1979. It was a colossal failure—big enough to discourage regular entrepreneurs but not passionate homebrewers with dreams.[1]

Enter Geoff and Marcy Larson. Geoff started his homebrewing hobby in college while earning his chemical engineering degree in the 1970s. He ran into his love, Marcy, while also realizing his dream of becoming a brewer of beer. Geoff apprenticed at Millstream Brewery in Amana, Iowa, and he studied brewing at the Siebel Institute of Chicago. Marcy worked to support them both.

They ended up in Alaska, and Geoff met legends such as Bert Grant and Matthew Reich at the first Great American Beer Fest in 1984. He even got a personal tour of the famous Anchor Brewing in San Francisco. It was time for Geoff and Marcy to start their own brewery in Juneau.

It was the first brewery since the debacle of Prinz Brau five years prior, and they had problems raising the funds for this crazy venture. Banks turned them down. Relatives turned them down. They found eighty-eight curious individuals to help them raise money and opened Chinook Brewery in 1985, which became Alaskan Brewing Company in 1990.

They were the second brewing license in the state, the first being Prinz Brau, and it was slow going at first. Being in such a remote state with low population, they had to import every beer-making material except for water. In 1985, the US Postal Service didn't mail directly between Juneau and Anchorage.

They persevered, becoming a huge, if not unlikely, success.

Microbreweries and brewpubs appeared all over the state in the 1990s, mostly on the highway system, from Anchorage to Fairbanks.[2]

As in the rest of the country, craft brewing has boomed in Alaska over the last ten years. With more than twenty-five breweries, an Alaskan brand was voted best US beer in a poll of forty-five hundred people at the Great American Beer Fest in 1988. Since water is a main ingredient in beer, some say the water from glacier ice is a factor in the quality of Alaskan breweries.

QUALITY OVER QUANTITY

As one of those great Alaskan brewers, Gabe Fletcher wanted to show his local community what a real beer festival should be like, highlighting beer from the continental forty-eight states for Alaskans to enjoy.

For the first two years, the Culmination Beer Fest was held at a performance center in Anchorage. When Anchorage Brewing built a new, larger facility, Fletcher held the beer fest at the brewery, both inside and in the parking lot.

The 2019 fest featured thirty-two breweries with four different beers each. The brewers bring their best—not normal or staple beers, such as ales, but exotic, special beers. Only a few beers are on draft and are placed on regular tap lines in the brewery. Most are in cans or bottles. This is because leftover beer in partially used kegs are a waste, while the bottles and cans can be saved and used later as a backlog of beers.

LOGISTICS TO THE FRONTIER

The logistics are extensive and expensive. Fletcher coordinates everything so that the beers come in fresh. Beers such as India pale ales are shipped overnight, right from canning. Sturdier beers are shipped separately on a truck. The timing is perfect so that beers are at their best and at just the right temperature.

Fletcher tries to bring in just enough beer so there isn't waste, although he does have pallets of cans and bottles from over the years. He recently got a license to sell those on-site at his brewery so that customers can enjoy this backlog of great beer.

Shipping to Alaska is insanely expensive. It costs $1,300 to ship six cases of beer.

Fletcher handpicks the breweries from all over the country, from Oxbow to Allagash. Each beer is expertly crafted, and he chooses only the best. The goal is for every brew to be amazing.

The Culmination runs from 2:00 to 6:00 p.m. on a Saturday. Due to weather and Fletcher's interest in outdoor activities, he's moved the festival around the calendar. In the first year, it was held in April. Then it moved from May to June to July, and then to August, and now later in July. Late July has the perfect weather and time for fishing in the ocean near Anchorage. Weather is also an issue due to half the fest being outside in the parking lot.

The festival brings beer in about thirty minutes before the attendees. Attendees get double-sided pamphlets with a list of beers to check off after sampling. They also receive a five-ounce glass each, and pours are three ounces. The festival provides people to pour so that the brewers don't have to. These pourers are educated in their assigned beers weeks before the event.

STAFF AND SAFETY

With the smaller size of 350 people and the intimate setting, the festival never gets crowded. There might be one or two in line at a booth, but even that is rare.

The brewery staff works at the festival, and there are also several volunteers. The volunteers must possess alcohol serving cards. Half or more of the volunteers return or have worked it before. Culmination provides floaters to give breaks to the pourers so that they can go around and try beers too.

Security is minimal with the relaxed crowd. The people at the festival are well behaved. An occasional patron imbibes too much and must be helped home, but those instances are rare.

No one drives to the Culmination, especially since the parking lot is full of breweries. Security at the event ensures that people get in cabs or are picked up.

The festival brings in portable toilets to help with the bathroom situation.

FOOD AND ENTERTAINMENT

The Culmination includes catered food, mainly pizza. One year, a friend drove up from Seattle with a pizza oven in the truck. That was a drive of 2,260 miles and forty-three hours to bring amazing pizza to the festival. Last year, Anchorage Brewing bought in its own pizza oven, and the same friend arrived with a batch of amazing meatballs to go with the pizza. People can eat as much as they want.

There are no competitions. Fletcher wants to keep it simple and intimate, and he thinks that competitions would make it too complicated.

The event includes live music, though. A jazz band plays inside the brewery. One year, the Culmination had a postfestival concert in the parking lot. They brought out kegs of a 2.8 percent alcohol by volume India Pale Ales for people to drink, and a stoner metal band played. It made for a long day, so they probably won't do it again.

AMAZING BEER AT THE EDGE OF THE WORLD

The festival has stayed the same, perfect size since the beginning. It sells out in minutes.

With its growing popularity, tickets have become increasingly difficult to get. Less than half of the attendees fly in for the festival. The people who come comment on how eye-opening and amazing it is, and they say the Culmination is the best festival out there.

One couple got engaged at the Culmination. Another group flew up as a bachelor party.

Brewers love coming up as well. They talk about the hospitality, how the fest is run, and the beauty of Alaska.

With Fletcher's focus on community and the importance of keeping it small, brewers stay and collaborate on a beer every year.

Most of the brewers also arrive as much as four days early. They all get together for drinks. Over the next two days, Fletcher takes them fishing on the ocean. They have a BBQ at his house, with fun and activities together through the week. During the one or two days following the festival, others go out hiking.

The fishing happens near the Gulf of Alaska, first on a big boat with several brewers. Then Fletcher takes another eight out on his smaller boat for more leisurely fishing.

He also takes a group out to check out the glacier and have a glacier martini. Back on the boat, they have oysters. It is a once-in-a-lifetime experience for most people.

The Culmination doesn't lose money, but it doesn't make any either. That's not the point. People need to keep the lights on, but Fletcher's passion is for people to get together and have a great experience. Those experiences create community, whether the experience is having a glacier martini or an excellent craft brew.

Great beer fests take work, but it takes extra work for someone in Alaska to bring in US breweries for a festival. It is difficult for Fletcher to get in touch with breweries and convince them to come to the festival, especially if they don't know who he is. Then he flies them in with cases of their beer. Some high-profile breweries aren't interested in coming to Alaska.

But no one in Anchorage or the state has the reach or friendships that Culmination does. The hard work pays off, not in "bigger and better," but in a friendly type of family reunion with brewers and drinkers, enjoying the great beer together.

What You Need to Know

EVENT Culmination Beer Fest

WEBSITE https://theculminationfestival.com/

LOCATION Anchorage Brewing Company, 148 S 91st Ave.,
    Anchorage, AK

FOUNDED 2013

DATES Late July

DESIGNATED DRIVER TICKETS AVAILABLE No

ADMISSION FOR THOSE UNDER TWENTY-ONE No

CHAPTER EIGHT

Hard Liver Barleywine Festival

Seattle, WA

THE HARD LIFE

The old cliché is that what doesn't kill us makes us stronger. It's also the mentality of the Hard Liver Barleywine Festival in Seattle. It's time to step up and drink the hard stuff . . . if you're strong enough.

Matthew Vandenberghe grew up in the United States, but his father's Belgian heritage influenced him, including giving him a taste for amazing beer.

It was difficult to find great beer in the United States, so Vandenberghe made his way to Belgium at the age of seventeen, enjoying the old cities and especially the brewpubs in the region. He took notes on the beers he sampled and loved.

Eventually, he moved from Eugene to Seattle. He began homebrewing, and then worked at Maritime Pacific Brewery. There he met Matt Bonney, a coworker. The two became friends, not the least in part due to their passion for beer. In 1998, they opened Bottleworks Brewery together.

More trips to Belgium (with Tim Webb's *Good Beer Guide to Belgium* in hand) further developed the pair's love of traditional European styles and Belgian culture in general. In 2005, they opened a new business, Brouwer's Café, not a brewery but a café based on the Belgian model of the local beer bar. With sixty-four taps, Brouwer's sprung from the vision of having a place for people to relax and enjoy amazing beers from all over the world.

The Good Beer Guide to Belgium was originally published in 1992 (with subsequent editions) and gave insight into different types of events held in Europe. Those ideas hovered in the back of Vandenberghe's mind when he and Bonney visited the Toronado Barleywine Festival in San Francisco, put

Glass of barleywine. *Photo by Todd Bradley.*
Courtesy of Brouwer's Café.

on by David Keene, whom they befriended. Vandenberghe and Bonney were impressed with the festival focused on barleywine and glad to see that the strong ale was treated with such respect. The Toronado put it on every tap handle.

The idea began to start a barleywine festival in Seattle, and the dream became a reality just after the turn of the century.

For the first two years, the Hard Liver Barleywine Festival was held at a nearby elementary school and the Phinney Neighborhood Center. These were successful events. Brewers came and poured their own beers, giving it an intimate and family-style feel.

Brouwer's Café opened in 2005, and the third annual Hard Liver was held on the new site.

Why the name Hard Liver? Barleywine is one of the strong ales and contains a high alcohol by volume (ABV) percentage. Keeping up with others while drinking these beers is considered a difficult task. The high alcohol content takes a toll on the liver, and the promise is that consuming and enduring this style makes people better and stronger.

When the Hard Liver began, 10 percent ABV was the legal limit in the state of Washington. Many of the high-quality world-class beers were above that limit, however, and so Vandenberghe and others fought to get the law changed. It eventually was.

HOP TO THE HISTORY OF BEER

The history of beer in Washington is a history of people and hops.

German-style light lagers from local breweries, such as Olympia and Rainier, ruled the late nineteenth century.

Olympia Brewing Company in Tumwater began in 1886. It was eventually sold in 1982 and shut down for good in 2003.

Several local breweries merged in the late nineteenth century, in character with the growing competition of larger breweries from Milwaukee and St. Louis. Breweries such as Bay View, Seattle Malting, and others combined resources to become Rainier Brewing. The first record of Rainier appears in 1883 in Georgetown, and they produced the most popular beer in the Northwest for fifty years. Competition with bigger brands brings national attention, and Ranier eventually sold to Pabst.

Washington passed statewide Prohibition in 1916. In May of that year, the police dumped twelve thousand quarts of beer from Rainier Brewing into

Selection of beers at the café. *Photo by Todd Bradley. Courtesy of Brouwer's Café.*

the bay. By the summer of that year, almost every Washington brewery had closed or gone out of business.

While Rainier was large enough to survive Prohibition and the Depression, the resurgence of brewing, specifically craft brewing, in Washington can be placed on the feet of two men, Charles Finkel and Bert Grant.

Charles Finkel loved the great beers from Europe and began importing them from Germany, UK, and Belgium, exposing the locals in Seattle to different styles and more complex flavors. Finkel opened Pike Brewing Company in 1989 and was best known for the XXXXX Stout, a nod to the English stouts. Redhook was the first brewery in Seattle, but Finkel and Pike had greater impact on the next generation of brewers.[1]

Bert Grant was born in Scotland; was raised in Toronto, Canada; and had settled in Yakima, Washington. He flaunted his Scottish roots, donning a kilt whenever he could. He brewed his ale for his own pleasure, and he made that clear.

Grant started testing and tasting at a Toronto brewery. Thirty years in US corporate beer wore on him, and Grant moved to Yakima. He tinkered with recipes until he made "the Ale Master." The perfect ale. Friends agreed that he achieved it and helped him open a brewery.

In July 1981, the state raised the limit to 8 percent ABV, and two weeks later, Grant's Scottish ale went out to local saloons. Grant continued to experiment with styles and opened the first brewpub in Washington since before Prohibition. He put the pub in an old railway station and held court at a table in the middle of the room well into his seventies. The pub closed soon after his death in 2001.

Grant has been credited with establishing the Northwest style of hoppier India pale ale, and he became a legend in the craft industry.[2]

Washington wasn't the first state with microbreweries, but it was where the movement found a welcome and stable home. Washington had its advantages. The cool, gray weather was good for sipping ale, and the state license law favored establishments with no liquor or low ABV (3.2 percent) beer. Washingtonians drank at taps. The imports were also already popular from Finkel's influence.

Hops was another advantage. Washington grows 70 percent of the hops in the country, and 20 percent of the world's. No wonder hops are an essential element to the Northwest hoppy taste and style.[3]

The first wave of Seattle craft brewing was exciting on a creative level. Brewers collaborated and competed for the best in hops and the best of the old styles with a new spin on tradition.

Seattle brewers operate on an informal apprenticeship model, the old tradition of learning from a brewmaster, and then moving on to another brewery. This led to the current resurgence of brewers.

TAKE ONE FOR THE TEAM

Brewers and beer lovers like Vandenberghe and Bonney.

Bonney eventually left to start his own business, a Toronado in Seattle, but the Hard Liver continues at the Brouwer's Café.

The Hard Liver celebrates barleywine. Several old ales, such as wheat wine, fall into that category. The Northwest beer style of barleywine tends to be more hoppy and less malty than the English version. The Northwestern and Western barleywine has its own unique taste for those reasons.

The festival moved to Brouwers Café in the third year, and it switched to all the beers being on the taps and poured by staff. During the festival, forty-five to sixty barleywines are on tap, depending on the year. The staff at Brouwer's does an amazing job with the provided draft list. The patrons get

Busy inside of the café during festival. *Photo by Todd Bradley.*
Courtesy of Brouwer's Café.

the draft list, numbered and in alphabetical order, and they can order four- or eight-ounce pours. "Number and size" is a phrase that is used several times during the festival.

Some groups of four try to go through all the barleywines over the course of several hours.

Everything is priced à la carte. Admission is free, but people must pay per drink. Vandenberghe thought about a ticketed system, but Washington's overserve laws make that dangerous. The pay-as-you-drink system helps with control and accountability. The café can adhere to serving standards and pace people as they usually do.

The café holds up to 250 people at a time, so it is first come, first serve on the days of the festival, and others are allowed in when people leave. A line starts before dawn, and once the festival opens midday, they reach capacity in twenty minutes. Patrons come and go, and the café sees between eight hundred and one thousand people a day.

The Hard Liver starts at 11:00 a.m. on Saturday and Sunday, either on the last weekend in February or the first weekend in March.

Handful of snifters. *Photo by Todd Bradley. Courtesy of Brouwer's Café.*

RISE TO THE MOMENT

Brouwer's Café means "brewer's bar." These are Belgian terms. There are two traditional types of cafés—brown and grand cafés. Brouwer's is a grand café, serving beers from all over the world, anniversary brews, and special brews from places such as Allagash Brewing Company. Brouwer's operates every day as a sixty-four-tap bar and restaurant, but for the festival, they change all the taps over to barleywine.

The Hard Liver is a professional beer event. They are attentive to everyone on an individual basis. It's not a huge crazy crowd that's difficult to manage. Servers are magnificent at getting several orders right at one time and getting beers to the people who asked and paid.

Patrons are limited to three orders at a time. The event is organized so that everyone can get beverages and the staff can constantly check on guests. The strength and heaviness of the beer helps drinkers take it slow instead of guzzling. It's not deceptively high in alcohol content like some brews.

At many beer fests, people stand in long lines with plastic cups for small samples. At Brouwer's, they use snifter glasses that capture the aroma of the beer and makes the experience far superior.

"Size and number" when patrons order. *Photo by Todd Bradley. Courtesy of Brouwer's Café.*

A person could drive by the festival and not know anything is going on. But if you go inside, it is a madhouse, going full speed for hours at a time.

BE STRONG

The Hard Liver does have a competition that drives a great deal of interest. They bring in professional judges to evaluate the beers in the back room. The judges blind taste and rate the beers. It takes a while, but they whittle it down to the top three winners. People wonder what is great. What should I try next? When winners are announced, those beers go fast!

What is so unique and special about barleywine? It's at the top of the strong ale list and remained an important style through history. It grew mostly in England but made it over with colonists to America, who then developed their own style, as they do with many things. Barleywine is synonymous with strong ale, and Vandenberghe believes in saving the old traditional styles.

The motivation for the Hard Liver was a celebration of strong beer and how unique a beer can be. It can be deep, strong, rich, and delicious. Even within the barleywine family, there is diversity and variety. Even Seattle has its own unique barleywine.

Another view inside Brouwer's Café. *Photo by Todd Bradley. Courtesy of Brouwer's Café.*

The selection at the festival is a little different each year. For example, the Hard Liver looks forward to Alaskan breweries coming down.

Barleywine is brewed longer and is heavy on malt and sugar, which makes it sweeter and gives it a higher ABV percent. Barleywine is aged in cellars for years and is often released as vintages from past years, much like the *wine* in its name.

Brouwer's is a restaurant with a full kitchen that leans toward Belgian cuisine with a Northwest American spin on it. During the festival, it develops a special menu with meats and potatoes that utilize barleywine in the recipes as much as possible. It makes the food rich and amazing.

TAKE RESPONSIBILITY

The only additional security on the days of the event is an extra employee at the door. The staff is constantly aware of service issues and will escort people out for a ride home if they feel it is necessary. There have been next to no issues, however.

Previous employees come back to help since they know the full-speed pace and difficulty of that day. New staff can have trouble remembering beers and several orders at once for long periods, so the veterans return. Like the barley-wine they serve and celebrate, serving during the festival isn't for the timid.

They use only the regular bathrooms at Brouwer's, since they designed and built the facilities with the café capacity in mind. There may be a slight line of one or two people, and the restrooms might need a little more maintenance during the festival, but with staff helping monitor needs and the patrons, bathrooms haven't been a problem. It's called the Hard Liver, after all. Just hold it, right?

TAKE HEART

The story of beer is the story of people, and the beauty of the craft industry is the personalities that have shaped it. Like a young man with a Belgian heritage falling in love with traditional styles and dreaming of a Belgian style grand café realized, which he realized at Brouwer's. Or a community in Seattle introduced to amazing imports and influenced by a Scottish American brewing legend. The explosion in Northwest craft brewing focused on regional ales, generously hopped and bold in flavor.

Look at barleywine. There is no better place than Seattle to celebrate an Old World strong ale and bring their own innovations to the style. The Hard Liver Barleywine Festival keeps the old traditions alive with a new generation of brewers, and everyone is welcome to the party.

If you can take it, that is.

What You Need to Know

EVENT   Hard Liver Barleywine Festival

WEBSITE   https://www.brouwerscafe.com/category/hard-liver
-barleywine-festival/

LOCATION   400 N. Thirty-Fifth St., Seattle, WA

CHAPTER NINE

Firestone Walker Invitational Beer Fest

Paso Robles, CA

PROGRESSIVE FEST

The craft beer industry is all about innovation, progress, and pushing the boundaries. That makes sense because it was born in California.

Known for its wine, California was also home to the hippie movement in the 1960s, a movement that was anti-establishment and pro-people. Those major social changes had several effects, one of them being the forward-thinking, community-driven people's movement of craft beer.

It is in character, then, that brewmaster Matt Brynildson scoffed when his friend Tom Madden approached him about starting his own beer fest at the Paso Robles Event Center. There were too many already. It had been done.

Firestone Walker Brewery is one of the top breweries in the country, recently ranked number five. It opened in 1996 and grew successful in the unlikely small town of Paso Robles in the middle of California's wine country. Brynildson and Firestone won the World Beer Cup in 2004, 2006, 2010, and 2012. The brewhouse in Paso Robles became a leader in the craft beer field.

Why not start their own beer fest? In Brynildson's mind, not only were there too many already, but the beer fest scene was developing into a series of messy drunk fests. The brewers often didn't even participate. Interaction with the artisans of brewing was a core belief in the craft culture.

Madden didn't give up. He asked Brynildson what a perfect festival experience would be like. Brynildson answered that it would include the best brewers from around the world, great local food, exceptional live music, air-freighting the beer, and ensuring that the brewers were in attendance and

The official Firestone Walker glass.
Photo by Nicholas Walker. Courtesy of Firestone Walker.

cared for. It should also be less snobby than the local wine fests but not a drunk affair, he said.

But it couldn't be done, Brynildson argued. They couldn't afford it.

Madden found a way to get the financing for a festival that lived up to Brynildson's dream. Special events manager Veronica Kral and the rest of the Firestone Walker events team found a way to organize the event.

The first year, Brynildson expressed his vision to everyone: a world-class festival with brewers who were leaders in the craft beer revolution. It would be a day where everyone put aside sales and marketing pitches and shared great beers and the stories surrounding them.

He even wrote down the simple rules. Brewers would bring special beers and the artisans who created them. Brewers, beers, good music, and the people who cared about them would work together for a great day.

THE FIRST SPARKS

The first brewery opened in California in 1849, one year before it became a state. Adam Shuppert Brewing opened in San Francisco 250 years after the first brewery in America did in Manhattan in 1612. The Gold Rush and rapid growth in San Francisco made it a great time and place to start brewing beer.

This meant Shuppert wasn't alone. Others followed. Hilbert & Borchers, Bavarian, Eagle, Albany, Railroad, Union, and more emerged in the next decades. Pacific Brewery, one of many of its day, later became the infamous Anchor Brewing.

Hops were introduced in California in 1854, and Sonoma County became a major hops supplier until Prohibition. By the late nineteenth century, "California hops" were famous in England.

German immigrants started the vast majority of California breweries, and they brewed the new lager beer style. However, unlike in places such as Wisconsin, California's weather didn't cooperate with the German brewing techniques, and refrigeration hadn't come all the way west yet. The brewers came up with California Common, a mix between the lager and English ale.

"Steam beer" was a cheap blue-collar brew that the heavy-drinking hard worker loved.

After the Gold Rush boom, the beer scene developed and changed. With new mechanical refrigeration and pasteurization, bottling advances, and railroads, some breweries consolidated to compete with larger breweries from the Midwest. From 1873 to 1910, the number of breweries in California

Slogans ready for the festival. *Photo by Nicholas Walker. Courtesy of Firestone Walker.*

declined from 4,000 to 1,500—although the production of beer grew 600 percent and saloons doubled from 150,000 to 300,000.

Saloons developed a reputation in California, as they did in the rest of the country. They were busy but populated with loud guzzlers. The valid association with illegal activity, used by saloons to compete and survive, didn't help.

The thirteen-year "noble" experiment of Prohibition closed most of the breweries in the state. Some made "near beer" (a nonalcoholic beer), sodas, or other products. The repeal gave hope for a short time but was met with the reality of the Great Depression. During and after World War II, stricter legislation made it difficult for new breweries. By 1967, the top four breweries of the country dominated the industry.[1]

Hope did come, though—first, in the form of a brewing program at the University of California, Davis in 1958. That program became a hallmark of homebrewing and new brewers trying to learn and open businesses in the coming decades.

A twenty-five-year-old beer lover came to California in 1965. Fritz Maytag, from the family that made washing machines, sat in a local pub and drank his favorite beer. The bartender told him to enjoy that beer since it might be his

Cheers from the attendees. *Photo by Nicholas Walker. Courtesy of Firestone Walker.*

last. The brew from Anchor Brewing would soon be out of business. Anchor made sour, bad beer, but Maytag was passionate about great beer.

Maytag bought a controlling interest in the brewery in 1967. Soon, he brewed artful, tasty beers. The brewery grew in business and popularity through California. It was the first "craft" brewery in the country. It kicked off a revolution.

The early 1970s saw a rebellion against the shrink-wrapped, stale consumer culture in America. California pioneered the charge. Much like Papazian in Boulder, Colorado, California was the perfect place and time to explore craft brewing.

Jack McAuliffe had visited Scotland and developed a taste for English ales. After stopping by Anchor Brewing, he built his own brewery in Sonoma, California, in 1977. It's regarded as the first modern microbrewery in the nation. McAuliffe named the brewery New Albion in honor of pre-Prohibition Albion Ale and Porter Brewing in San Francisco. New Albion didn't last long but influenced many brewers in the region.

In 1980, Ken Grossman, who owned a shop that sold supplies for home-brewers, made his way to Anchor and New Albion. Those breweries, along with Maytag and McAuliffe, inspired Grossman. Grossman took welding lessons to manufacture his own brewing equipment and built Sierra Nevada Brewery. His pale ale created a new style of American beer.

The notorious law that made brewpubs illegal was repealed in 1982, a landmark for craft brewing in most states. More breweries opened.[2]

In 1990, there were fewer than seventy breweries in California. By 2000, two hundred had opened. In 2013, the governor signed the bill that allowed sales of growlers, glass containers that could be filled at the brewery and taken home. One year earlier, in 2012, fifty-four countries and four thousand beers competed in ninety-five categories at the World Beer Cup. California breweries won fifty-five medals, more than any state—and even more than any country.

Today, in 2019, there are more than nine hundred breweries in California, more than in any other state. The state boasts 39.5 million people, and 95 percent of them live within ten miles of a craft brewery.[3]

THE FIRE SPREADS

The first brewery in California may have been 250 years behind the first in America, but brewing has exploded in the state with a vengeance.

The brewers invited to the Firestone Walker Invitational are the most innovative and skilled brewers in the world. They are either longtime friends of Brynildson's or people who met him while he was traveling. In order to be included in the festival, the head brewer or lead brewing staff must come and serve beer, ensuring that the attendees have an opportunity to meet the beer makers and learn more about the beers and the brewery. It's all about the brewers.

The first Firestone Walker Invitational was a one-of-a-kind event. Brynildson handpicked well-respected breweries, such as Bells, Three Floyds, Founders, Sun King, and Revolution. Being an international event with the vision of featuring beer from all over the world, Mikkeller from Denmark and Yo Ho from Japan were also at the first festival.

Forty breweries came to the first one on Saturday, June 9, 2012. The event lasted from 1:00 to 6:00 p.m. at the fairgrounds, with music on the stage. The crowd started gathering at the entrance by eleven o'clock. The People's

Bands rock out at the festival. *Photo by Nicholas Walker. Courtesy of Firestone Walker.*

Choice awards are a big part of the event, and Three Floyds Dark Lord was voted People's Choice beer that year.

In the second year, the temperatures rose to one hundred degrees or more. The festival provided plenty of water, shade, large fans, and mist makers to keep the patrons cool and hydrated. Live music included the bands Hot Buttered Rum and White Buffalo. It was a unique event where hipsters, beer nerds, and cowboys all gathered, relaxed, and had the best beer in the world, with more than forty breweries that year and twenty food offerings from local restaurants.

Year seven saw temperatures of up to ninety-nine degrees, but that didn't keep the beer lovers away. More than fifty-five breweries were represented in 2018, with a wide range of beer styles. With another roster of breweries handpicked by Matt, the brewers were a dream lineup for beer geeks.

Another stage on a beautiful California evening. *Photo by Nicholas Walker. Courtesy of Firestone Walker.*

KEEP THE FIRE GOING

The Firestone Walker Invitational has a staff of ten on the core team. They work to add more value and excellence every year. As an example, 2018 was the first year they had a Kickoff Concert. Nikki Lane and Mother Hips played for the folks, and the event has become a favorite of the festival.

Garage Project from New Zealand was one of a few breweries that included carrot cake as an ingredient in a beer. Interestingly, Garage Project also won the People's Choice. The People's Choice for food was Eureka! Burger from the local county of San Luis Obispo. They served twenty-eight-day aged sliders.

In the eighth year, 2019, more than twenty-five hundred beer fans attended the festival, a good number for a town of thirty-one thousand. The tickets

The friendly crowd at the Firestone Walker. *Photo by Nicholas Walker. Courtesy of Firestone Walker.*

sold out in a minute or less. A VIP ticket allows entry one hour earlier, and a large portion of the VIP ticket sales goes to the festival's charity, Paso Robles Pioneer Day.

With better weather and beautiful eighty-one-degree temperatures, attendees enjoyed sixty breweries in 2019. The People's Choice was the Bruery, but there wasn't a bad beer to be had all day.

The events team spends months planning every detail, from getting the beer to Paso Robles, to brewer lodging, and mapping which brewer goes where in the venue. The event team takes into account the needs of the brewers. Do they need a draft trailer? Jockey boxes? All of that coordination takes a great deal of time.

Then they come up with activities during the event, from the bands to Behind the Beer sessions where brewers are interviewed. The events team chooses food and beer pairings, especially with special beers. Much of this information is included in the official Invitational App—the schedule, a map, and information on every beer being served.

During the actual week of the festival, all staff works with volunteers to set up tents, hang signs, and more. Now that they've reached their eighth year, the team is a machine, with people who know their roles and execute them with excellence.

Chefs are stationed throughout the Robles Event Center. Everyone receives a plate on the way into the festival, and the food is complimentary all day. Many note the high quality of the food, which is equal to the beer.

The festival hires a security company to work with the event staff, and both teams work together to make judgment calls. Firestone Walker provides complimentary transportation to local hotels to ensure than no one is drinking and driving after the festival is over. Fortunately, there haven't been any issues over the years.

RELIEF FROM THE HEAT

It's all about the brewers. The heat of Paso Robles bears down on people in the summer months, so the festival traditionally rents the local water park for the brewers on a separate day, complete with a lazy river, giant slides, and a wave pool. Since the festival rents it out, the park allows beer throughout the entire facility, the only time of year that happens. Nothing is better than drifting down a lazy river with a can of Pivo.

The night before the event, the brewers are invited to a traditional Central Coast Santa Maria Style BBQ with live music. It is a relaxing time to have a sense of community and gather with brewer friends around the world before the big event kicks off the next day.

This past year, 2019, twenty-nine chefs and restaurants brought delicious food for the event. The People's Choice competitions make sure that everyone—brewers and food vendors—brings their A game, which only brings more value to the attendees.

The Paso Robles Pioneer Day benefits from the success of the festival. The nonprofit Pioneer Day works to preserve the hometown of Paso Robles, and friend Tom Madden works for them as well.

PASSING ON THE FLAME

The positive feedback from attendees praises the event. Media lists the Firestone Walker as one of the best beer fests every year. Despite the success and great reputation, the events team adds new elements every year to improve

Amazing food options for the attendees. *Photo by Nicholas Walker. Courtesy of Firestone Walker.*

it. The ability of the events team to organize and execute an event so complicated and extensive blows Matt Brynildson away every year.

The heart of the Firestone Walker Invitational is to gather like-minded, forward-thinking brewers from around the world to commune and network. Matt takes pride in providing a comfortable environment for them to showcase their art and passion with a limited but knowledgeable fan base. Then the magic happens.

Who knows what the next creative ingredient, like carrot cake, might be? But in a craft brew culture and industry where innovation has been foundational, a festival in progressive California is sure to blow minds and start new conversations about what might be possible.

The answer is anything. Anything is possible.

What You Need to Know

EVENT Firestone Walker Invitational Beer Fest

WEBSITE https://www.firestonebeer.com/brewery
/invitational-beer-fest.php

LOCATION Paso Robles Event Center, 2198 Riverside Ave.,
Paso Robles, CA
About three hours south of San Francisco International Airport on
US 101 or about three and a half hours north of Los Angeles Airport
on US 101 or I-5

FOUNDED 2011

DATES Late May to early June

DESIGNATED DRIVER TICKETS AVAILABLE No

ADMISSION FOR THOSE UNDER TWENTY-ONE No

Pinup girls and brews.
Photo courtesy of Tony Bennett Photography.

CHAPTER TEN

Tailspin Ale Fest

Louisville, KY

SPREADING WINGS

On Thursday night, Tisha Gainey got the call she would always remember.

The first Tailspin Ale Fest was taking place on Saturday. Standing near the airplane hangar where it would be held, Tisha looked over at the sunset. Anxiety and excitement rose within her, normal for something new and big. She answered the call from Trevor Cravens, her friend and cofounder of the beer fest.

They sold out. She smiled with relief and pride as Trevor shared that not only had they sold out, but people had registered from other states, from farther away than they had expected.

The idea, the dream, began a year or more earlier. Both Tisha and Trevor had experience in the beer industry. Tisha worked as a local craft beer representative in Louisville and later shifted to a new job as a beverage director for restaurants. She always advocated for craft beer and had been to a few beer fests in her day.

Trevor's involvement with *Draft Magazine*, a nationally distributed publication about craft beer, meant that he had also experienced different beer festivals through the years.

Both had craft beer friends in Louisville. While some local festivals existed, Louisville lacked a real signature beer fest. The idea for a new beer fest came together over a beer at a bar, as many ideas do.

The venue became the first question. Tisha had looked at a local airplane hangar for her wedding and thought it would make a great spot. Bowman Field is the oldest continually operating commercial airfield in the United

---

States, even though Louisville's Muhammed Ali International Airport is only five minutes away. Bowman holds an historic treasure, however—a World War II–era airplane hangar with historic information, an icon for Louisville. As a bonus, Bowman sits in central Louisville, near the entertainment district.

They had the perfect location.

Trevor and Tisha reached out to friends in the beer industry, keeping the festival focused on all-American craft beer and recognizing local Kentucky breweries.

The World War II airfield made the branding and theme simple. Vintage planes were already on display, and they hired women to dress as pinup girls for attendees to take pictures with.

They sold sixteen hundred tickets in the first year (2014) with only the hangar as the footprint. They picked a date in February between the Super Bowl and March Madness, when not much was going on in town. February in Louisville can be cold or warm. That first year, the sun came out, and the temperature rose into the sixties.

COACH CLASS BEER

Early brewers in Lexington organized as proprietorships or partnerships, with two or three workers each. Those early companies used ingredients from local farmers and processed them at the breweries.

They produced porters and common table beers with top-fermenting yeast, which they aged and served at room temperature. Those who brewed added hops as a preservative, making a full-bodied and bitter beer.

John Nancarrow opened the first commercial brewery along the Kentucky River in Woodford County in 1789. Four years later, he relocated to Lexington and renamed it the Lexington Brewery. It operated for decades but was bought and sold several times.

As was the case in the rest of the country, Kentucky didn't avoid the influx of German and Irish immigrants in the mid-1800s, who arrived with their love of beer. In Kentucky, those from the Irish or German culture tried to reproduce the beer of their homelands, but in the state's warm weather, they produced a low-alcohol thirst-quenching beer, an American cream ale.

Soon, the brewers in the state produced a dark cream ale with six-row malt, native corn, and dark and caramel malts as ingredients. This brew came to be known as Kentucky Common.

Most of the beer brewed in Kentucky was in the northern part of the state, near Cincinnati.

George Wiedemann Brewing Company began in 1870 and became the largest brewery in the state. Wiedemann closed in 1927 but reopened in 1933. The brewery made it through Prohibition and the Depression, and but large brand competition closed it in 1967. It has made a resurgence in 2011, however.[1]

Falls City Beer has, surprisingly, survived since 1905, calling itself Louisville's first craft beer.[2]

Kentucky Common was most popular among the labor class. It was quickly available and cheap to produce. Brewers delivered it to market while it was still fermenting in the barrels; it would finish by the time it was served. From brewery to consumer took only six or eight days.

The short shelf life of Common probably contributed to the limited range of its popularity, but it continued as the go-to beer until Prohibition. As an example of its popularity, in some parts of Kentucky, 75 percent of the beer sold was Common. Prohibition killed Kentucky Common and most of the breweries in the state.

The craft beer movement brought Kentucky Common back in modern and traditional styles. The traditional style is sourer than the modern.[3]

Despite being a bourbon state, Kentucky has seen its share of craft breweries, even decorated ones. Bluegrass Brewing Company opened in 1993 and has won several medals at the Great American Beer Fest over the past twenty years.[4]

WHEELS UP

Tailspin organizes breweries by distributor for purely practical reasons. It hasn't been a problem for people to find the beers they want and allows for better supply to the breweries. Brewers from Kentucky have their own section. Along with a map, large signs show people where the breweries are.

Part of Tisha and Trevor's mission was to elevate beer to the same level as wine, spirits, or any other beverage, such as bourbon. This was a big challenge, but with forty-seven state breweries in Kentucky, the craft scene is making headway and bringing attention to the breweries and their high-quality beers.

As experienced people in the craft industry and running other festivals, Tisha and Trevor are always trying to improve the guest experience at Tailspin. That usually comes down to details, such as knowing where to park or

Festival in the hangar. *Photo courtesy of Tony Bennett Photography.*

not running out of beer. Over time, they've added more components. One addition is the shuttle that takes people to local spots and breweries. People can get to those restaurants or pubs, have a pint and a bite before the fest, and then get a safe ride to and from the event.

To further encourage safe drinking and driving, the festival allows people to park at the airfield and leave their cars overnight.

Tailspin has grown to five thousand people since 2014. This has resulted in increased security and diligence relating to the behavior and accountability of the guests. Fortunately, it is a well-behaved crowd.

The festival markets itself as a sampling and discovering event, not an "all you can drink" time. They invite attendees to come in and find new beers, sample styles or brews they haven't tried before, and take their time. The festival doesn't want any empty booths, and talking to the brewers is encouraged.

Most of the breweries—90 percent—have brewers or employees present. Conversations abound at the booths about what is in each beer. The environment includes some waits and short lines at stations.

IN-FLIGHT ENTERTAINMENT

Activities around the festival entertain the attendees as well. Along with the opportunity to take photographs with airplanes and pinup girls from the 1940s motif, there is live music. The live music isn't just a sideshow— high-quality bands play.

Another fun element is the silent disco. Attendees exchange their IDs for headphones. The color of the headphones determines which of the two DJs they will listen to. Then the patrons enter a four-thousand-square-foot dance floor, which is fenced off from the rest of the event. It is interesting to see a large crowd of people dancing without hearing the music, unless you have headphones too.

One year, Nappy Roots, a Kentucky rap group, joined the fun and rapped along with the silent disco DJs.

Enjoying the Silent Disco. *Photo courtesy of Tony Bennett Photography.*

Since cider and sour beer fall under malt drinks in Kentucky law, the festival has a dedicated bar for those drinks, along with meads. Tailspin is located in bourbon country, and there is another dedicated area for bourbon barrel ales and beers.

The festival gives a respectful nod to the aviation community while at the historic Bowman Field, which those from that community enjoy.

FIRST-CLASS FEST

At the heart of Tailspin is a passion for craft beer. Tisha fell in love with great beer in the 1990s and has worked in the craft industry since 2007. With the inclusive and community nature of craft beer, Tisha has seen more females in the craft industry recently, which is impressive and welcome.

With that passion for craft beer in mind, Tailspin is for both beer geeks and newbies and ensures both feel welcome. The 2019 festival included seventy-five breweries and more than two hundred styles at the festival. The sponsor and featured breweries have participated since the first year, and many breweries bring special beers—taproom only or limited release with the only keg in Kentucky. Guests look for those. The Kentucky breweries are very popular, and people love to support them. New Belgium is a crowd favorite for their great beers that aren't available anywhere locally.

Tailspin Ale Fest falls close to Sweetwater Brewing's anniversary. They make a cake for Sweetwater every year, and Tailspin gets their anniversary beers first.

Braxton Brewing Company collaborated with an ice cream company in Cincinnati and made ice cream floats with the beer they brew together. It was very popular!

MORE THAN PEANUTS

Pallets of free bottled water are offered to keep attendees hydrated. For designated drivers, free coffee is available from a local shop.

Many of the same food trucks have come back for six years. These are local trucks that are accessible for patrons to purchase from, each one with a different kind of food.

Most of the 250 volunteers return each year to assist at the festival. Non-brewery personnel does much of the pouring because of state liquor laws, and they are a critical part of the operation. Tailspin tried a separate party for the volunteers, but they had so much fun at the actual event that few showed up.

The fest gives them a T-shirt and feeds them. The volunteers love the festival and that it supports a great local charity.

Dare to Care serves twelve counties in Kentucky and donates nineteen million meals a year to needy families. Tailspin supports the charity, and as Tailspin organizers learn more about Dare to Care, they try to find more ways to help. They've leveraged the event to increase giving every year. Donated prizes were raffled last year; 100 percent of the proceeds went to the food bank.

Tailspin organized more giving by selling paper steins at local businesses throughout the city. Local breweries that are connected with Tailspin also give to Dare to Care. West Sixth Brewing in Lexington makes a Pay It Forward beer, a Cocoa Porter that they sell for six months, and a percentage of sales goes back to Dare to Care.

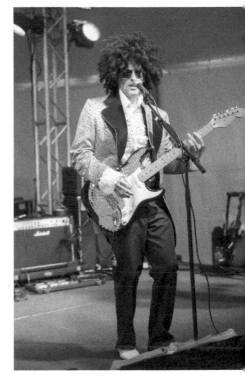

Live music for the crowd.
Photo courtesy of Tony Bennett Photography.

OVER THE TOP

For those who purchase VIP tickets, Tailspin goes above and beyond. VIPs get in one hour early, and the package includes a food voucher at any of the food trucks. A special gift bag, provided by Yelp, with swag from featured breweries and partners comes with the VIP ticket. A snack bag from a local potato chip company is included in the bag. The VIPs enjoyed a custom-embroidered football scarf in 2019.

A local homebrew competition determines the official Tailspin ale for the year. The competition began in the second year with a local homebrew club named the Lagers. Partners judge the competition to pick the best homebrew. The winner can brew the beer on a pro system and be the official Tailspin ale, which is available only at the festival. Awards for first, second, and third are awarded during the festival.

The mayor of Louisville comes to the festival and makes a speech. It is nice to get support from the city.

Those who attend love the entertainment, the silent disco and live music, but they come back for the beer. The beer reps and the beer list—all if it makes it special. Tisha spends time ensuring that the festival gets the best breweries and special beers.

All the small components come together for a great festival. The only complaint has been bathroom lines.

While year one saw great weather, year two brought seventeen degrees and ice and snow. The restrooms were kept underneath a massive tent, men's and women's back to back, and some people didn't see the row of portable toilets behind it. Long lines formed, but once attendees were guided to the portable toilets, the situation improved.

A local company lined a shipping container with troughs of thirteen urinals and called it Urination Station for the guys. The men are encouraged to save the portable toilets for the women.

BEYOND THE HORIZON

What's next for the Tailspin Ale Fest? They have considered adding another session. The festival sells out every year, and physical expansion isn't possible since they've filled the current space. However, adding another session would be extra work, and there's just Trevor and Tisha.

Whether or not they add the extra session, with Trevor and Tisha's commitment to quality, improvement, the local community, and the importance of relationships, there is little doubt that the Tailspin Ale Fest will continue to soar.

What You Need to Know

EVENT Tailspin Ale Fest

WEBSITE http://tailspinalefest.com/

LOCATION Bowman Field, Louisville, KY

FOUNDED 2014

DATES Early March

DESIGNATED DRIVER TICKETS AVAILABLE Yes

ADMISSION FOR THOSE UNDER TWENTY-ONE No

CHAPTER ELEVEN

Prairieland Beer and Music Festival

Wichita, KS

WIDE OPEN SPACES

Sometimes being one of the last ones on a group text means you get the job.

Emily Boyd co-owns Central Standard Brewery, a brewery in Wichita, Kansas. The local breweries in Wichita support each other, and it is a great community to be a part of. Three years ago, a group text went to many of the breweries, suggesting that Wichita should have its own beer fest. At a meeting, Boyd accepted the responsibility to serve on a small planning committee to discuss the topic.

Wine people organized the other main beer fest in town. It wasn't as local, and it was more distributer driven.

The brewers who were interested in the beer fest had participated in others, many of which were fundraisers or competition focused. While fun, they were not what the brewers loved most.

What if they took what they loved about beer fests and held one in Wichita? It would be a beer fest by brewers, for brewers. It would include the owners, brewers, and their beers. They would invite those who were super passionate about beer, and brewers would bring special offerings. Also, it would benefit the local brewers' guild.

They decided to hold the festival outdoors in the fall, and great music would be a big part of it. They started looking for a facility that would work.

Fortune smiled. A new outdoor music venue opened downtown that was a perfect match. The first Prairieland Beer and Music Fest was held at the WAVE music venue.

FROM BAD TO GOOD GROUND

Brewing found a difficult home in Kansas. The fight over whether Kansas would be a free or slave state dominated the hearts and minds of the people, and that struggle in the state became a leading cause of the Civil War. Once the military conflict ended, it wasn't long before Temperance started having influence. Beginning in 1881, laws were passed limiting or prohibiting alcohol in the state; Prohibition lasted until 1948, longer than in any other state. Laws prohibiting liquor continued until 1986, erasing the last of the old laws.

Kansas took in the immigrants from Germany, just as the rest of the country and territories did in the mid-1900s. With unsafe water and little else to drink, the light German beers swept the state. In Girard, a town in Southeast Kansas, there was a saloon for every nine houses. The area was known as the Little Balkans, as many had emigrated from that European region. The local coal miners kept those saloons busy.[1]

By 1860, brewing was Kansas's fourth biggest industry and led to ninety breweries. Leavenworth had a large German American population and boasted six brewpubs in the mid-nineteenth century.[2]

Kansas Brewing Company was the first to open in the territory in 1854. Muehlebach Brewing Company came soon after, in 1869. A conglomerate of local breweries joined to form Kansas City Breweries Company, and Imperial Brewing produced a popular regional brand. In 1901, the largest pre-Prohibition brewery west of the Mississippi River was Heim Brewing Company, well known for its German lagers. Hailing back to their German Oktoberfest heritage, the Heim brothers started an amusement park for the community.

A proponent of Temperance, John St. John, was elected governor in 1879, and laws prohibiting alcohol soon followed. Prohibition ended the breweries in Kansas. Muehlebach survived, but Schlitz bought it out later in the 1900s.

The legal breweries might have their closed doors, but Temperance couldn't close the Kansas City party scene. Speakeasies and jazz joints continued until 1933.[3]

For many years of Kansas's Temperance laws, alcohol was still legal in Missouri. When Prohibition became federal, bootlegging and medicinal loopholes existed to fill the gap and the demand.

The pharmacy industry boomed during Prohibition. Druggists could sell alcohol to anyone who signed a statement of illness and disease, with no doctor's prescription needed. Alcohol treated rheumatism, diarrhea, asthma, and other ailments. A vegetable compound for "feminine troubles" contained 18 percent alcohol.[4]

The statewide Temperance effort to curb the "cowboy culture" continued to make it illegal to brew and sell on the same premises. As seen in other states, that discouraged the growth of local craft breweries, but the law changed in 1986.[5]

Even today, Kansas is one of a few states where grocery stores are prohibited from selling wine and spirits and any beer over 3.2 percent alcohol.

Thirteen years after the law changed, Chuck Mageri opened Free State Brewing Company in Lawrence, an early brewing success. New breweries are opening, and there are now more than thirty in the state.[6]

THE NEW FEST

Boyd co-owns one of those breweries, Central Standard. She and the other brewers involved in planning Prairieland envisioned a festival where brewers felt celebrated and would bring their A games, with special, unique beers and even brews that they didn't have in their own taprooms.

Forty-five breweries came in 2019, along with local wine, cider, kombucha, and cold-brew coffee. Most of them are Kansas breweries, but some are from the surrounding states of Missouri, Nebraska, Oklahoma, and Arkansas. These breweries don't distribute in Wichita but make collaboration beers with local brewers. It is a great opportunity for relationship building between the brewers and further collaborations between them.

Some of the breweries involved are Boulevard, Defiance, Blind Tiger, and the Free State Beer. Central Standard brought out the last keg of beer that won a gold medal at the Great American Beer Fest, something special for the patrons.

At the WAVE, ten-by-ten tents line the perimeter of the lawn area. A few are placed in the middle as well.

THE SOUND OF THE SKY

With the word "music" in the name, music is an important aspect of the event. The bands play an eclectic mix of genres—wild blue grass, New Orleans party funk, and a Latin band of students from the local university as examples. Music plays indoors from 3:00 to 6:00 p.m., and then the bands move outside for the evening at 6:00 p.m. and go until 10:00 p.m.

THE BOUNTY

Prairieland brought in food trucks the first year, which was on WAVE's opening weekend. None of the venue's concessions were ready yet. The kitchen was fully operational in 2019, so WAVE provided the food, especially a nacho dish people enjoyed.

GOOD NEIGHBORS

WAVE puts on big shows all year long, and they provide their own security. They can handle the beer fest. The venue is one block from a major trolley line that runs all day, and it's central to the part of the city where attendees can walk.

Along with sufficient security, WAVE also has bathroom facilities rated to serve three thousand people, more than enough for the seven hundred in attendance for the festival.

A local animal rescue charity, Beauties and the Beast, supplies the volunteers who work the festival. The rescue organization brings puppies that are up for adoption to play with at the event, and two were adopted in 2019. The volunteers run ice and buckets and check with breweries to make sure they have everything they need.

Beauties and the Beast works with other breweries as well, and it has been a great partnership. The proceeds from Prairieland go to Beauty and the Beast and the local craft brewers guild.

To keep it simple and focused on the brewers, there aren't any competitions. Organizers sought feedback for this young festival from the brewers. How could they make it better for them? They gave great feedback and loved that the brewers were made to feel like rock stars.

NO PLACE LIKE HOME

While they've added a couple more people to the planning committee, it is still a small group, including Boyd, and the Prairieland hasn't developed into the well-oiled machine others have become over years or decades.

The festival has been successful, however—not only on the bottom line but in connecting with breweries and in bringing value to the city. As a native from Wichita, Boyd enjoyed hosting her brewing friends and showing off the town to them.

That is the heart of the craft beer culture—innovation, collaboration, support, and friendship. As a co-owner of her own brewery, Boyd brought those elements to the Prairieland Beer and Music Festival, where you can come, hang out, have some great beer, hear excellent music, and play with a puppy or two—and maybe even take one home.

What You Need to Know

EVENT Prairieland Beer and Music Festival

WEBSITE http://prairielandfest.com/

LOCATION 650 E. Second St. N., Wichita, KS

FOUNDED 2018

DATES Mid-September

DESIGNATED DRIVER TICKETS AVAILABLE No

ADMISSION FOR THOSE UNDER TWENTY-ONE For music portion only

CHAPTER TWELVE

Brews on the Bricks

Hays, KS

THE BREWER FOUNDATION

While the Brews on the Bricks festival has a VIP ticket, Sara Bloom makes it clear that the brewers are the VIPs. Without them, there wouldn't be a festival.

The town of Hays, Kansas, rolls out the red carpet for the brewers. The night before the festival, Friday night, the festival partners with Gella's Diner and Lb. Brewing to host a reception. Lb.'s opens the back room for an exclusive brewers' party to wine, dine, and thank them. The brewers can sit in a relaxed environment, where others serve them, and talk shop with their peers. They receive swag bags full of items from the community. One year, when the festival was on May the Fourth, Star Wars Day, they received inflatable lightsabers.

At the event the next day, the festival provides water, ice, pitchers, a separate bathroom for the brewers, and volunteers to give the brewers breaks.

Bloom works at the Downtown Hays Development Corporation. After visiting a beer fest in another state, one of the thirteen board members wondered why Hays wasn't hosting a beer fest. The rest of the board agreed and created the event.

The first step was contacting the breweries in Hays to figure out the event, catering, and promotion. Two breweries helped organize the festival and get it off the ground. Those brewers served on the event committee to bring suggestions and trends to help provide aspects that brewers would love and make them want to come back.

Special cornhole design for Brews on the Bricks. *Courtesy of Downtown Hays Development Corporation.*

Brews on the Bricks limited tickets to four hundred in the first year, wanting to start slowly and ensure an excellent experience for everyone. They didn't want to get too big too fast. The downtown area is called the Bricks, and the organizers leased out the major parking lots from the city for that Saturday afternoon. There were fifteen breweries in the first year.

TAKING IT ON THE ROAD

Now in their fourth year (2019), they sell out the two thousand available tickets and bring in more than forty breweries.

Most of the breweries are from Kansas, Colorado, Missouri, and Nebraska. A few are from around the world. The organization is a mix of all the breweries.

Only a select 250 tickets are VIP tickets. The VIP ticket holders enter at 12:30 p.m., an hour and a half earlier than general admission, for a private tasting of beers that features a variety of foods brought in by eight restaurants. Beer and foods, from desserts to beef sticks to tacos, are paired together.

Lb. Brewing pouring for the patrons. *Courtesy of Downtown Hays Development Corporation.*

General admission begins at 2:00 p.m. and lasts until 6:00 p.m. Many of the same vendors and food trucks set up so that people can purchase food. Brews on the Bricks tried something different in 2019. They mixed the vendors and food trucks in with the breweries—three breweries, and then one food vendor and so on. Part of the event is under a large tent, and several food trucks set up outside of it.

The festival is an outside event on the street, so rain, wind, and freezing temperatures can appear and cause complications. People keep coming back. However, due to the freezing temperatures one year, they moved the festival from the end of April to the beginning of May.

People around the Happy Basset Brewing Company. *Courtesy of Downtown Hays Development Corporation.*

THE HEARTBEAT OF THE CITY

The event uses forty volunteers, and many of them return. Volunteers help with check-in, security, and general work through the event. They come from the local community, most of them to support the downtown area and the value to the community. Fort Hays State University sends students from their tourism and hospitality group. These young men and women are interested in learning more about event planning and management.

The official security is composed of officers from the Fort Hays Justice Department. Some of them use the event as part of their police training.

Uber is a sponsor, and the festival partners with them for drop-off and pickup. Brews on the Bricks has a great designated driver booth with water, ices, root beer, cream soda, and other nonalcoholic offerings from the breweries. It is important to Bloom and the organizers that everyone gets home safe.

The event brings in several portable toilets—one for every ten people! That's the formula they've found that works best.

Music is absent from the early VIP experience to allow for more conversation and connection. The live band comes on at 2:00 p.m. with the general admission.

Attendees can play on eight cornhole boards for further entertainment.

Brews on the Bricks held a homebrew competition, put on by the local Hays Homebrew Club, from 2017 to 2019. The club approached the festival about the competition. The winner could brew a giant batch of the winning beer at Lb. Brewing.

The Hays Homebrew Club wants to expand and grow the competition. Since the festival doesn't have the margin or time for that extra work, the competition will be its own event after 2019. The homebrewers will still help at the fest in the future, especially by offering some special samples at the VIP experience.

Music to entertain the attendees. *Courtesy of Downtown Hays Development Corporation.*

The Downtown Hays Development Corporation is nonprofit, and the Brews on the Bricks raises funds for their organization, which helps develop and support local businesses and grow the quality of the downtown area.

Red velvet cheesecake as part of the great food that is available. *Courtesy of Downtown Hays Development Corporation.*

Play cornhole with a brew in hand.
Courtesy of Downtown Hays Development Corporation.

THE PEOPLE IN YOUR NEIGHBORHOOD

People come from all over the country, but most attendees hail from Western Kansas. Being close to Colorado, people in Western Kansas love beer, and the opportunity to try great beer and breweries is a draw.

The patrons enjoy the VIP ticket for the early admission and the food pairings with the homebrew samples, which are unique. The mix of breweries and food trucks garnered positive comments from the general attendees too.

The organizers send surveys to the brewers, and they invite everyone who is involved in the event—vendors, volunteers, security, and breweries—to a meeting. They ask for feedback on what was good and bad and what could be improved.

This input helps Bloom and the Development Corporation tweak the event. They don't want it to be the same from year to year. Including a surprise or two makes it interesting and keeps people coming back. For a small town of twenty thousand people and two breweries, it's been a great event.

The star of the show, however, is the beer. The brewers and their creations drive the event, which brings the patrons and the brewers back. It celebrates amazing beer, from those who brew at home to local pros. The gathering takes to the street on the Bricks of Hays, and attendees look forward to next year when they can do it again.

What You Need to Know

EVENT Brews on the Bricks

WEBSITE https://www.downtownhays.com/events-1
/brews-on-the-bricks

LOCATION Tenth Street between Main and Fort Streets,
Hays, Kansas, about four hours west of Kansas City on I-70

FOUNDED 2011

DATES Late August

DESIGNATED DRIVER TICKETS AVAILABLE? No

ADMISSION FOR THOSE UNDER TWENTY-ONE No

CHAPTER THIRTEEN

Savor Beer Fest

Washington, DC

LIVING THE DREAM

Great beer is worth celebrating all by itself. But the attraction of the craft beer movement isn't about great beer alone. It's about community, connection, and sitting at one big table in the center of the room instead of at small tables in the corners. Craft beer culture is related to the movement in America for quality and the support of local establishments with character. When people go out, they want their beer, music, restaurants, and coffee to have stories and to be served by others with a dream.

It is no surprise, then, that so many beer fests feature music, food, and even coffee. These are not chain companies but local specialty vendors with the same commitment to quality and local character. Adding these elements enhances the enjoyment of great beer.

For those who dive headlong into craft or homebrewing, the complex flavors, styles, and innovation are fundamental parts of their love story with beer. What better way to celebrate those flavors than to pair beer with amazing food?

The Brewers Association, the same organization responsible for the Great American Beer Fest (GABF), started looking for a way to give the public a way to experience and learn about pairing craft beer with amazing culinary dishes.

At the same time, Washington, DC, was in its "nation stage" of developing a viable craft beer scene. As is the pattern in so many states and stories, legislation has important effects on the development of craft beer. When the Brewers Association and those representing the craft industry made their

Official Savor glass.
Courtesy of Brewers Association.

The crowd at the Savor. *Courtesy of Brewers Association.*

appeals to their representatives, an event showing the value and culture of craft beer made sense as well.

The Savor, an American Craft Beer and Food Experience, began in 2007.

Adam Duyle, the executive chef with the Brewers Association, which also heads up Paired at the GABF, picks ten other award-winning chefs to work with breweries and pair the beers with dishes. Duyle finds out what beers each brewery is sending to Savor. With one hundred breweries from around the United States, this is a daunting task.

The next step is a gathering of experts in the Colorado area to taste the beers and do some initial exercises, asking questions such as "When you drink this beer, what are you thinking? What is the umami? What are the foods you'd like to see?" Once those comments are recorded, the ideas are narrowed down to a menu to offer guidance to the chefs to pair and design dishes.

SIPPING THROUGH HISTORY

The early brewers in the area brewed the English ales and porters from their British culture. An English style brewery (Andrew Wales Brewery) existed in 1770, six years before the Revolution. Cornelius Cunningham opened the first brewery in DC proper in 1796, but it closed less than fifteen years later.

Those English brews were heavy in the heat. As they did in the rest of the country, German light lagers came to save the day. German lagers were designed in a colder climate, and the warmer weather made lager brewing difficult.[1]

Robert Portner, from the city of Alexandria, Virginia, started a revolution of his own by inventing ice-making machinery in the 1870s. Now German lager could be brewed year-round. Perhaps it was no accident that he started Robert Portner Brewing Company soon after, and his brewery grew to be the largest in the South.

With the lighter, lower-alcohol German lagers and the advancement in technology through refrigeration and transportation, beer became the national drink once the Civil War ended.

In early twentieth-century Washington, DC, a few brands dominated the local market. Christian Heurich Brewing Company brewed several different styles and produced the most beer in DC. Christian Heurich was also the only DC brewery to survive Prohibition.

Beer suffered the most under Prohibition. Bootleggers found spirits and liquor more profitable, and as a result, the tastes of alcohol drinkers changed. Those Americans who did drink beer gravitated to the corporate giants with advertising. Due to that competition, Heurich closed its doors in 1956.

The watershed moment in most states occurred in 1991 in DC—the legalization of brewpubs, which allowed breweries to produce and serve on the same premises. Capitol City Brewery opened in the first part of the 1990s and won several medals at the Great American Beer Fest.[2]

The explosion of craft beer over the last decade can be seen in DC as well. Port City opened in 2011, along with Brau, Three Stars, and Chocolate City. DC may have been in the "nation stage" in 2007, but the district has made up for lost time. It is twenty-seventh among the states in population but twelfth in the number of breweries in the United States and twenty-second in breweries per capita.[3]

RELISH THE CRAFT BREWS

How much of that growth is part of what is going on around the country, and how much is due to Savor? That's hard to tell, but Savor has sold out every year, keeping the number of tickets at around twenty-five hundred due to the

Pairing the food and beer. *Courtesy of Brewers Association.*

venue, the National Building Museum. The museum has iconic columns and a historic feel, and the lights at night create a beautiful environment.

Being at the National Building Museum makes the Savor a more upscale event than most beer fests. However, there is no dress code, so people wear everything from cargo shorts to tuxedos.

Savor is not a sit-down dinner. Attendees receive a series of small plates with the samples of beer. Areas to sit or stand while people eat are available, but the festival encourages meeting the celebrity brewers and talking with those behind the pairings about why certain foods were paired with certain beers.

The doors open at 6:00 or 7:00 p.m., depending on the year, and the event goes until 10:00 p.m. on a spring night in May. The focus is to highlight the interplay between beer and food. The music is only for background.

Patrons are encouraged to be responsible, and with two-ounce sample pours and plenty of food, overconsumption is never a problem. To be safe, the museum's location near transit stops and other forms of public transportation makes it easy to be responsible.

The brewers work the event to educate and serve their beers. Only a small number of volunteers help the Brewers Association staff. Because of the pairing focus, there aren't any competitions.

The bathrooms at the museum are sufficient for the event. There is no need to bring in extra portable toilets.

A DELIGHT FOR THE TASTE BUDS

Savor sells out a month or so in advance. When people arrive and register at the event, they receive tasting glasses and a program that includes a menu. Attendees can plan their journeys through the evening depending on which beers or food they'd like to begin with. Would they like to start with light beers and work up to barrel-aged? Or perhaps they could start with appetizers and create their own meal experiences. It is fully up to the individuals to explore as they like.

A great night for couples. *Courtesy of Brewers Association.*

Pairing oysters with the beer. *Courtesy of Brewers Association.*

There are a couple of beers and two pairings at every brewery station. Lines are typically small.

As a more upscale festival with a pairing focus, Savor proves to be a great date or couples' night. Sometimes groups of friends share the experience together too.

People come year after year, traveling from other states and planning trips, and they often say this is their favorite event. Commemorative beers are made especially for the event, and the attendees get a bomber-size bottle of them to take home.

The VIP ticket includes a dedicated entrance and an earlier start time with a private meet and greet with the brewers. The VIPs enjoy a private area with special extra pairings for them, and they leave with a special gift at the end of the night.

Savor is popular with the brewers. Not only do they enjoy the conversations and the evening but also see their great brews paired with amazing food, which makes it even more enjoyable for those artists. The supporting breweries include Allagash from Portland, Maine; Bells from Kalamazoo, Michigan; and Crazy Mountain from Denver, Colorado.

Friends on the Savor journey together. *Courtesy of Brewers Association.*

For some examples of pairings, Allagash's Barrel and Bean, a wood- and barrel-aged strong beer, was paired with a coffee and chocolate whoopie pie. Atlas Brew Works' Blood Orange Gose was paired with Choptank oysters. Monday Night Brewing's Pervasive Species, an American sour ale, was paired with grilled lamb, peas, and feta.

La Cumbre Brewing came from Albuquerque, New Mexico, and their Sun Fode, an India pale ale, was paired with goat cheese, pistachios, strawberries, and a white balsamic. Port City Brewing from nearby Alexandria, Virginia, brought their Franconian Kellerbier, an unfiltered German lager, and the chefs paired it with corn hush puppies and pink peppercorn aioli.

ENJOY THE QUALITY AND THE COMPANY

Savor combines the best of craft beer with the best food, and it is designed as an amazing experience that everyone enjoys. People can try every pairing, so there is enough food and beer for everyone, but the focus is on sharing the quality of brews and dishes, producing a flavor explosion that puts smiles on everyone's faces and keeps them coming back every year for more.

What You Need to Know

EVENT Savor Beer Fest

WEBSITE https://www.savorcraftbeer.com/

LOCATION The Anthem, 901 Wharf St. SW, Washington, DC

FOUNDED 2011

DATES Mid-May

DESIGNATED DRIVER TICKETS AVAILABLE No

ADMISSION FOR THOSE UNDER TWENTY-ONE No

CRAFT BEERS

Conclusion

MAKING FRIENDS. GATHERING WITH PEOPLE FOR A SHARED EXPE-
rience creates lasting memories.

Along with the passion for great beer, those early homebrewers invited
their friends over to share the beers and get feedback in basements, garages,
and kitchens. At its heart, craft beer isn't about drinking alone; it is about
hanging out and connecting over a great beer.

The conversation might start with the flavor of the beer, the recipe, the
mash, when the hops went in, and more. But the conversation moves on from
beer to family, friends, jobs, dreams, life. It's about time slowing down and
enjoying new and old relationships.

Beer fests are the ultimate evolution of that culture. Sure, there are some
that get out of hand with drunken attendees, but the ones the brewers and
beer geeks love are those that continue with the heart of crazy young people
who became legends in their own time—Maytag, Grossman, Grant, Papazian, and others.

They weren't trying to be legends, though. They were trying to change
things and make life taste better. They changed laws. They changed an
industry.

There are other fests that aren't included in this book. As Art Larrance said
in the foreword, you can find them in many small towns and big cities. They
are each unique. This book celebrates only a few.

As someone of Irish and German descent, my ancestors were among those
who emigrated from Europe, brought their beer culture, innovated and grew,
and felt the brunt of anti-immigrant ire. But the craft story is one of inclusion.

That message is still as current ever, with political and cultural clashes and divisions dominating headlines and extremes on either side.

Maybe it's in my Irish German DNA, or maybe it's my personality. Maybe I'm like the millions of others in the United States who are tired of the barking back and forth. There's something attractive to sitting down with a well-crafted brew and beginning the conversation as friends. Wherever it goes from there, it appears to me that we will arrive at a better place.

This has been my experience over the years with homebrewers, the people who open breweries near me, and those whom I've interviewed to write this book. They are amazing, resilient, principled people who are generous dreamers. I hope that has been your experience at a beer fest. If you've never been to one, I highly recommend making the effort to attend one of the ones in this book. You'll have excellent beer and a great day.

And possibly make a friend.

NOTES

INTRODUCTION

1. "History of the Oktoberfest," Oktoberfest International Guide, accessed November 1, 2019, https://www.oktoberfest.net/history-oktoberfest/.

2. Maureen Ogle, *Ambitious Brew: The Story of American Beer* (Orlando: Harcourt, 2006), 15–17.

3. Greg Voakes, "How Beer Saved the World," *Huffington Post*, last updated October 16, 2012, https://www.huffpost.com/entry/how-beer-saved-the-world_b_1354789.

4. Ogle, *Ambitious Brew*, 161, 174, 187.

1. SUWANEE BEER FEST

1. Michael Lundmark, "How Beer Single-Handedly Saved the State of Georgia," *Suwanee Magazine*, May 4, 2015, https://suwaneemagazine.com/whats-brewing-3/.

2. Bob Townsend, "The State of Beer in Georgia," *Atlanta Journal-Constitution*, June 22, 2018, https://www.ajc.com/entertainment/dining/the-state-beer-georgia/8bIPcVR12pxjTO xrorib9O/#.

2. GREAT AMERICAN BEER FEST

1. Amy Zimmer, "Colorado Beer and Breweries," *Colorado State Publications Blog*, Colorado Virtual Library, June 19, 2019, https://www.coloradovirtuallibrary.org/ resource-sharing/state-pubs-blog/colorado-beer-and-breweries/.

2. "History of Colorado Craft Beer," Colorado Craft Beer Hall of Fame, accessed November 1, 2019, https://coloradocraftbeerhalloffame.com/pages/history-of-colorado-craft-beer.

3. Rich Wagner, "GABF Memories: Denver Festival Celebrates 21st Birthday," *Mid-Atlantic Brewing News*, October/November 2003, http://pabreweryhistorians.tripod.com /MABNOcto3GABF.html.

3. OREGON BREWERS FESTIVAL

1. Bob Woodward with Laurel Bennett, "The History of Oregon Beer," *1859 Oregon Magazine*, January 1, 2019, https://1859oregonmagazine.com/live/food-drink/oregon-beer -history/.

2. Joseph Rose, "Throwback Thursday: The History of Craft Beer in Oregon," *Oregon*

Live, January 1, 2019, https://www.oregonlive.com/history/2015/11/history_of_craft_beers
_in_oreg.html.

4. FESTIVAL OF BARREL-AGED BEER

1. Lisa Grim, "A Brief History of Beer in Chicago," Serious Eats, last updated August 9, 2018, https://drinks.seriouseats.com/2012/01/beer-history-chicago-diversey-siebel-meister
-brau-miller-lite-goose-island.html.

2. "Chicago Breweries," Chicagology, accessed November 1, 2019, https://chicagology
.com/breweries/

3. Greg Smith, "The Chicago Beer Riots," BeerHistory.com, accessed November 1, 2019, http://www.beerhistory.com/library/holdings/greggsmith5.shtml.

4. Chicagology, "Chicago Breweries."

5. Grim, "Brief History."

6. "How Prohibition Created the Mafia," History Channel, video, accessed November 1, 2019. https://www.history.com/topics/roaring-twenties/how-prohibition-created-the-mafia
-video.

7. Chicagology, "Chicago Breweries."

5. BREWGALOO BEER FEST

1. Karl E. Campbell, "Beer and Breweries," NCpedia, 2006, accessed November 1, 2019, https://www.ncpedia.org/beer-and-breweries.

2. Bryan LeClaire, "Beer in North Carolina," NCpedia, 2010, accessed November 1, 2019, https://www.ncpedia.org/culture/food/beer.

3. Daniel Harris, "State of Growth: The Rise of North Carolina Beer," *All About Beer Magazine*, June 14, 2015, http://allaboutbeer.com/state-of-growth-the-rise-of-north-carolina
-beer/.

6. GREAT TASTE OF THE MIDWEST

1. Kevin Damask, "The Original Beer Boom: The History of Brewing Runs Deep in Area," *Juneau County Start-Times*, January 10, 2017, https://www.wiscnews.com/juneau
countystartimes/news/local/the-original-beer-boom-history-of-brewing-runs-deep-in
/article_d0f63a3f-f344-578c-b414-4445801526fe.html.

2. Maureen Ogle, *Ambitious Brew: The Story of American Beer* (Orlando: Harcourt Books, 2006), 4, 15.

3. Damask, "Original Beer Boom."

4. C. H. M., "Why Milwaukee?," BeerHistory.com, accessed November 1, 2019, adapted from a discussion in Thomas C. Cochran's The Pabst Brewing Company: History of an American Business, 1948, https://www.beerhistory.com/library/holdings/milwaukee.shtml.

5. Ogle, *Ambitious Brew*, 30, 31.

6. Damask, "Original Beer Boom."

7. CULMINATION BEER FEST

1. David James, "Account of Alaska's Beer Booms Quenches Thirst for a Boozy History," *Anchorage Daily News*, last updated September 28, 2016, https://www.adn.com/we-alaskans
/article/account-alaskas-beer-booms-quaffs-thirst-boozy-history/2015/09/06/.

2. Tom Acitelli, "When Brewing Returned to Alaska—and Stayed," *All About Beer Magazine*, June 26, 2015, http://allaboutbeer.com/alaskan-brewing-history/.

8. HARD LIVER BARLEYWINE FESTIVAL

1. "The History of Beer in Seattle," *Seattle Magazine*, November 27, 2018, http://www .seattlemag.com/article/history-beer-seattle.

2. Eric Scigliano, "Here's to Washington's 35-year-old Craft-Brewing Industry," *Seattle Times*, October 12, 2017, https://www.seattletimes.com/pacific-nw-magazine/cheers-to -beers/.

3. Scott Hewitt, "'Washington Beer' Delves into Highly Hoppy History," *The Columbian*, November 30, 2019, https://www.columbian.com/news/2016/aug/13/washingtons-highly -hoppy-history/.

9. FIRESTONE WALKER INVITATIONAL BEER FEST

1. "History of Craft Beer in CA," California Craft Brewers Association, accessed November 1, 2019, https://www.californiacraftbeer.com/ca-craft-beer/history-craft-beer-ca/.

2. Ben McFarland, "The Oxford Companion to Beer Definition of California," *Craft Beer & Brewing*, accessed November 1, 2019, https://beerandbrewing.com/dictionary/ T6zmDiI95A/.

3. California Craft Brewers, "History of Craft Beer in CA."

10. TAILSPIN ALE FEST

1. Lexington History Museum, "Early Breweries," LexHistory, accessed November 1, 2019, http://lexhistory.org/wikilex/early-breweries.

2. "The State of American Craft Beer—Kentucky," American Craft Beer, February 3, 2016, https://www.americancraftbeer.com/the-state-of-american-craft-beer-kentucky/.

3. Nick Carr, "Kentucky Common: An Indigenous American Beer Style," Kegerator, January 8, 2018, https://learn.kegerator.com/kentucky-common/.

4. Lexington History Museum, "Early Breweries."

11. PRAIRIELAND BEER AND MUSIC FESTIVAL

1. Beccy Tanner, "Despite Kansas' Historical Roots, a Growing Number of Breweries in Kansas," *Wichita Eagle*, December 26, 2015, https://www.kansas.com/news/state/article 51732160.html.

2. "Kansas Could've Had a Great Beer History," F5 Paper, accessed November 1, 2019, http://f5paper.com/article/kansas-couldve-had-great-beer-history.

3. "A Brief History of Brewing and Distilling in Kansas City," Visit KC: Visitors Meetings (blog), February 4, 2019, https://www.visitkc.com/2019/02/04/brief-history-brewing-and -distilling-kansas-city.

4. Tanner, "Despite Kansas' Historical Roots."

5. F5 Paper, "Kansas Could've Had."

6. Tanner, "Despite Kansas' Historical Roots."

13. SAVOR BEER FEST

1. Warren Willis, "The State of American Craft Beer—Washington, D.C.," *American Craft Beer,* December 1, 2017, https://www.americancraftbeer.com/state-american-craft-beer -washington-d-c/.

2. Mark Jones, "D.C.'s Illustrious Brewing Past and Present," Boundary Stones: Weta's Local History Blog (blog), August 18, 2014, https://blogs.weta.org/boundarystones/2014 /08/18/dcs-illustrious-brewing-past-and-present.

3. Willis, "The State of American Craft Beer."

BIBLIOGRAPHY

Acitelli, Tom. "When Brewing Returned to Alaska—and Stayed." *All About Beer Magazine*, June 26, 2015. http://allaboutbeer.com/alaskan-brewing-history/.

American Craft Beer. "The State of American Craft Beer—Kentucky." February 3, 2016. https://www.americancraftbeer.com/the-state-of-american-craft-beer -kentucky/.

"A Brief History of Brewing and Distilling in Kansas City." *Visit KC: Visitors Meetings* (blog). February 4, 2019. https://www.visitkc.com/2019/02/04/brief -history-brewing-and-distilling-kansas-city.

California Craft Brewers Association. "History of Craft Beer in CA." Accessed November 1, 2019. https://www.californiacraftbeer.com/ca-craft-beer/history -craft-beer-ca/.

Campbell, Karl E. "Beer and Breweries." NCpedia. 2006. Accessed November 1, 2019. https://www.ncpedia.org/beer-and-breweries.

Carr, Nick. "Kentucky Common: An Indigenous American Beer Style." Kegera-tor. January 8, 2018. https://learn.kegerator.com/kentucky-common/.

Chicagology. "Chicago Breweries." Accessed November 1, 2019. https:// chicagology.com/breweries/.

C. H. M. "Why Milwaukee?" BeerHistory.com. Adapted from a discussion in Thomas C. Cochran's *The Pabst Brewing Company: History of an American Busi-ness*. 1948. Accessed November 1, 2019. https://www.beerhistory.com/library /holdings/milwaukee.shtml.

Colorado Craft Beer Hall of Fame. "History of Colorado Craft Beer." Accessed November 1, 2019. https://coloradocraftbeerhalloffame.com/pages/history -of-colorado-craft-beer.

Damask, Kevin. "The Original Beer Boom: The History of Brewing Runs Deep in Area." *Juneau County Start-Times*, January 10, 2017. https://www.wiscnews

.com/juneaucountystartimes/news/local/the-original-beer-boom-history-of
-brewing-runs-deep-in/article_dof63a3f-f344-578c-b414-4445801526fe.html.

F5 Paper. "Kansas Could've Had a Great Beer History." Accessed November 1,
2019. http://f5paper.com/article/kansas-couldve-had-great-beer-history.

Grim, Lisa. "A Brief History of Beer in Chicago." *Serious Eats*, August 9, 2018.
https://drinks.seriouseats.com/2012/01/beer-history-chicago-diversey-siebel
-meister-brau-miller-lite-goose-island.html.

Harris, Daniel. "State of Growth: The Rise of North Carolina Beer." *All About
Beer Magazine*, June 14, 2015. http://allaboutbeer.com/state-of-growth-the-rise
-of-north-carolina-beer/.

History Channel. "How Prohibition Created the Mafia." Video. Accessed November 1, 2019. https://www.history.com/topics/roaring-twenties/how
-prohibition-created-the-mafia-video.

"The History of Beer in Seattle." *Seattle Magazine*, November 27, 2018. http://
www.seattlemag.com/article/history-beer-seattle.

"History of the Oktoberfest." Oktoberfest International Guide. Accessed November 1, 2019. https://www.oktoberfest.net/history-oktoberfest/.

Jones, Mark. "D.C.'s Illustrious Brewing Past and Present." *Boundary Stones:
Weta's Local History Blog* (blog). August 18, 2014. https://blogs.weta.org
/boundarystones/2014/08/18/dcs-illustrious-brewing-past-and-present.

LeClaire, Bryan. "Beer in North Carolina." NCpedia. 2010. Accessed November
1, 2019. https://www.ncpedia.org/culture/food/beer.

Lexington History Museum. "Early Breweries." LexHistory. Accessed November 1, 2019. http://lexhistory.org/wikilex/early-breweries.

Lundmark, Michael. "How Beer Single-Handedly Saved the State of Georgia."
Suwanee Magazine, May 4, 2015. https://suwaneemagazine.com/whats
-brewing-3/.

McFarland, Ben. "The Oxford Companion to Beer Definition of California."
Craft Beer & Brewing. Accessed November 1, 2019. https://beerandbrewing
.com/dictionary/T6zmDiI95A/.

Ogle, Maureen. *Ambitious Brew: The Story of American Beer*. Orlando: Harcourt
Books, 2006.

Rose, Joseph. "Throwback Thursday: The History of Craft Beer in Oregon." *Oregon Live*, January 1, 2019. https://www.oregonlive.com/history/2015/11/history
_of_craft_beers_in_oreg.html.

Scigliano, Eric. "Here's to Washington's 35-year-old Craft-Brewing Industry." *Seattle Times*, October 12, 2017. https://www.seattletimes.com/pacific-nw
-magazine/cheers-to-beers/.

Smith, Greg. "The Chicago Beer Riots." Beer History. Accessed November 1,
2019. http://www.beerhistory.com/library/holdings/greggsmith5.shtml.

Tanner, Beccy. "Despite Kansas' Historical Roots, a Growing Number of Brew-
    eries in Kansas." *Wichita Eagle*, December 26, 2015. https://www.kansas.com
    /news/state/article51732160.html.
Townsend, Bob. "The State of Beer in Georgia." *Atlanta Journal-Constitution*,
    June 22, 2018. https://www.ajc.com/entertainment/dining/the-state-beer
    -georgia/8bIPcVR12pxjTOxrorib9O/#.
Voakes, Greg. "How Beer Saved the World." *Huffington Post*, October 16, 2012.
    https://www.huffpost.com/entry/how-beer-saved-the-world_b_1354789.
Wagner, Rich. "GABF Memories: Denver Festival Celebrates 21st Birthday."
    Mid-Atlantic Brewing News, October/November 2003. http://pabrewery
    historians.tripod.com/MABNOct03GABF.html.
Willis, Warren. "The State of American Craft Beer—Washington, D.C." *Ameri-
    can Craft Beer*, December 1, 2017. https://www.americancraftbeer.com/state
    -american-craft-beer-washington-d-c/.
Woodward, Bob, and Laurel Bennett. "The History of Oregon Beer." *1859 Oregon
    Magazine*, January 1, 2019. https://1859oregonmagazine.com/live/food-drink
    /oregon-beer-history/.
Zimmer, Amy. "Colorado Beer and Breweries." *Colorado State Publications Blog*.
    Colorado Virtual Library. June 19, 2019. https://www.coloradovirtuallibrary
    .org/resource-sharing/state-pubs-blog/colorado-beer-and-breweries/.

M. B. Mooney was in the second grade when his teacher, Mrs. Green, tried to keep him out of trouble by saying, "Why don't you write me a story?" He thought that was the best idea ever, and it has kept him out of trouble ever since. Mooney writes fiction and nonfiction and loves a good brew while he works, whether it's specialty coffee or craft beer, which is the basis for the writing podcast, Brew & Ink. He lives with his amazing wife, three creative kids, and a dog in Suwanee, Georgia.

Check him out on his website: www.mbmooney.com

Listen to the podcast: www.brewandink.com

Follow on Instagram @authormbmooney and Facebook— www.facebook.com/MooneyMB

EDITORS Ashley Runyon & Anna Francis
MARKETING MANAGER Stephen Williams
PROJECT MANAGER Darja Malcolm-Clarke
DESIGNER Pamela Rude
COMPOSITOR Tony Brewer